Dangerous Steps

DANGEROUS STEPS

Vernon Tejas
and the Solo Winter Ascent
of Mount McKinley

Lewis Freedman

Stackpole Books

Published by
STACKPOLE BOOKS
Cameron and Kelker Streets
P.O. Box 1831
Harrisburg, PA 17105

Printed in the United States of America

First Edition

10 9 8 7 6 5 4 3 2 1

Front cover photograph by Frank Fischbeck
Back cover photograph by Vernon Tejas
Cover design by Laura M. Pollack

"Mount McKinley Conquered by New Route," by Bradford Washburn, appeared in the August 1953 issue of *National Geographic*. Used with the permission of *National Geographic*, Washington, DC 20036.

Library of Congress Cataloging-in-Publication Data

Freedman, Lewis.
    Dangerous steps: Vernon Tejas and the solo winter ascent of Mount
McKinley/Lewis Freedman.—1st ed.
      p. cm.
    ISBN 0-8117-2341-0
    1. Mountaineering—Alaska—McKinley, Mount. 2. Tejas, Vernon.
3. Mountaineers—United States—Biography. 4. McKinley, Mount
(Alaska)—Description and travel. I. Title.
GV199.42.A42M323 1990
796.5'22'092—dc20
                                                    90-35027

Dangerous Steps

Acknowledgments

The author wishes to thank all the people who contributed their time and help to this project. Special thanks go to Donna Freedman.

Of Heroes and Dreams

The cowboy was the first truly American hero. And the myth of the cowboy, rather than the harsh reality of lonely life on the range, endures in the American mind. The cowboy of the half-hour television show and the movie western was a rugged, self-sufficient individualist, somewhat of a loner.

There is something of the cowboy in the heroism we applaud in the modern-day adventurer. In this century of exploration we have often found ourselves gasping with disbelief and cheering with enthusiasm for the man who stands out from the crowd, who goes where no others have gone. We stand in awe of those who risk their lives, who take bold new steps into unknown frontiers, and come back to tell us their stories. We hang on every word and live vicariously through their adventures.

Heroes are as varied as used cars, but not as numerous. They do not come in six-packs. They are not packaged in bushels, auctioned in stockyards, or sold on lots. Genuine heroes are as rare as the whooping crane, as elusive as Halley's Comet, and as distinctive and impossible to clone as snowflakes.

History must hang well on a hero for him to live on unblemished. These days we still seem to recognize George Washington, the father of our country, as a hero. We call Charles Lindbergh a hero because of his solo flight across the Atlantic in the *Spirit of St. Louis*. John F. Kennedy, however, seemed more of a hero in the aftermath of his assassination in 1963 than he does now.

In an age of both microscopic media inspection and disillusionment, heroes seem harder than ever to come by, or even to recognize. The author who titled his mid-1980s book *Hulk Hogan, America's Hero* wasn't taking any chances. We can laugh at such hyperbole about a professional wrestler, but it is also true that sports heroes in recent years have been unmasked as mortals, have become seen as just folks with special skills. It used to be that exceptional skills alone made such a figure a hero, but the more the individual was demystified, the more ordinary he seemed.

The standards for heroes have always been idiosyncratic. A few years ago, the magazine *U.S. News & World Report* published a survey of 315 men and women aged eighteen to twenty-four who were asked to name their heroes. The top ten drew heavily from the world of entertainment. Clint Eastwood was rated number one, and Eddie Murphy, number two. Then-President Reagan finished third. The rest of the top ten: Jane Fonda, Sally Field, Steven Spielberg, Pope John Paul II, Mother Teresa, Michael Jackson, and Tina Turner.

Heroism is truly in the eye of the beholder.

When purchasing a used car, the shopper must be wary and wise enough to look beyond the paint job and under the hood. In searching for heroes, one must be conscious of style parading as substance. So many seem attractive; so few will endure.

Have those acclaimed as heroes done something to be admired? Have they handled themselves in an exemplary way? Webster's New World dictionary defines a hero as "any person admired for his qualities or achievements and regarded as an ideal or model."

Perhaps we need to look for heroes in context. It seems fair to say that a hero should at the least be inspiring. Does this mean someone who rescued a child from a burning building? Or does it mean someone who won five Olympic medals? Or can it be both?

In searching the world for heroes of substance—a search for

ideological purity, so to speak—one can find reasons to put forward or eliminate almost anyone. We find ourselves admiring two types of people, though. The first is the truly selfless individual who gives of himself for the betterment of society. The second is the athlete who pushes his body to the boundaries of human endurance. To say that they are heroes is too simplistic, but to say that they have done something heroic is not far-fetched.

Put aside the selfless individual, the rare Mother Teresa, and consider just the concept of athlete as hero. It seems that these people have a huge capacity to inspire multitudes. Athletes who achieve the impossible, who find new limits for the body, do what we can only imagine, or even what we can't imagine. They test limits we can only hope to understand.

In Alaska there is a long-distance sled-dog race called the Iditarod. Every year mushers race dog teams more than 1,100 miles from Anchorage to Nome over the incredibly tough, frozen heart of the Interior. Each year there is a poster designed by Alaskan artist Jon Van Zyle printed to commemorate the race. The slogan on the 1983 poster reads, "Alone on the crest of your dreams."

Perhaps dreams explain what it is all about for those who explore the world for us, who climb the highest mountains and explore the moon and planets. In living their dreams, they act out ours.

There are no real limits, only places the body has never been before. "Ultimate challenges" last only until the next challenge comes along. Just remember how far 26 miles and 385 yards used to seem. That was before everyone's next-door neighbor ran the Boston or New York marathon. Just remember how impossibly high 29,028 feet seemed. That was before jet planes routinely flew higher. And that was before Mount Everest, which is exactly that height, was first climbed.

These days there are 3,000-mile bicycle races across the United States. There are Iron Man Triathlons and double Iron Man events. There are 210-mile wilderness cross-country ski races. All of the 26,000-foot Himalayan peaks have been climbed, and one man, Reinhold Messner, has climbed them all.

Man, it seems, has done everything, gone everywhere. The ultimate road trip was to the moon, but who knows where the next generation will go? Mars? Saturn?

But having exhausted all manner of challenge, having explored virtually every place on earth, man is not content to rest and pretend there is nothing left to do. He seeks new horizons, new challenges, new and more difficult ways to do things that someone else beat him to. If he can't do it first, then he might as well do it differently. Perhaps that is the modern endurance athlete's motto.

Doing something by oneself that only a group had heretofore achieved is one new way. We still have a place reserved in our hearts for that lone cowboy, out there on the edge, doing for himself and by himself, surviving by his own wits against the elements. For all our technological development, we recognize that nature is still the primary force of the universe, that for all our technological advancement and penetration of inaccessible places, there remain places where nature is still in charge.

Perhaps more than any other society, Americans admire the solitary individual. We like to think we can do things on our own, that we can rely on ourselves, that we are strong enough to survive if we have to without another's help. Yet at the same time we are a very social people, generally seeking safety in numbers, rarely venturing out on our own. We prefer the company of others and the security others give us.

Most of us will never seek a grand prize on one of the great mountains of the world. We lack the strength, the ability, or the courage; we recognize that, and are content living our routine existences. And those of us who do seek to challenge our bodies in any significant way rarely think of doing it solo, are rarely willing to consider risking everything completely on our own.

Because we are such social animals, our admiration for the solo achiever is magnified. It is enough for most of us to try to imagine climbing a huge mountain, or sailing a long distance on the open ocean with friends and assistance. It is beyond most of our realms of experience to imagine doing it alone. The stakes are upped so significantly.

In 1978, Messner climbed Nanga Parbat, a Himalayan mountain 26,650 feet high. He had already lost his brother on this peak on a previous trip. He had just been divorced. He sought solitude to conquer solitude.

Of course, choice of dreams, just like choice of heroes, is very personal. Jill Merriman, an Alaskan ultramarathon runner, looks

4

very hard into her own soul when she takes her body to new levels, to new places. "Running really teaches you what pain is all about," she once said. "You go out and run a hundred miles and every cell in your body hurts."

It was Merriman's dream to complete the Western States 100 Endurance Race, the foot race through California wilderness regarded as one of the toughest in the world. She did it. Imagine doing anything with every cell in your body hurting: That speaks of commitment.

We admire pluck. We admire discipline. We admire the will it takes to realize a dream. One-hundred-mile races may not be the dream of someone you know, but somewhere there is common ground that makes us appreciate what another human being has done. Her dream may not be our dream, but we recognize the realization of another's dream when it is fulfilled, and we applaud.

There is no underestimating the power of dreams. Dreams keep us going, and heroes make dreams come alive for all of us.

It was the dream of Anchorage mountaineering guide Vernon Tejas to become the first man to succeed at climbing Mount McKinley alone in the winter. In the winter of 1988, he did it. Something in the style, the manner, the drama of how he defied the winter elements, of how he defied death on the tallest mountain in North America, touched the many.

Tejas's dream became a dream for the world to applaud.

Denali

Mount McKinley. Denali. The High One. The Great One.

Great and white, great and mighty, Mount McKinley bespeaks power and eternity. It is a hulking mass of forbidding darkness and stunning light. It is both bringer of life and harbinger of death. So blindingly bright in its whiteness, so menacingly intimidating in its dark shadows.

It is a magnet for men who dream, a magnet for men who should know better. A teasing lady who often is no lady, McKinley lures and seduces. It flirts with men who can't say no to its beauty. It crushes men who respond to the invitation, but stay too long.

Mount McKinley is wilderness man's obsession. Sometimes it is loving and gentle with that obsession. Sometimes it is a cruel, demanding, and mean mistress who can strip men down to their trembling souls and make them run for a cover they can't find.

To Alaskans it is the symbol of the country, the wild, untamed, beauty of their land. It stretches 20,320 feet into the sky, sometimes touching the sky, sometimes disappearing in the sky.

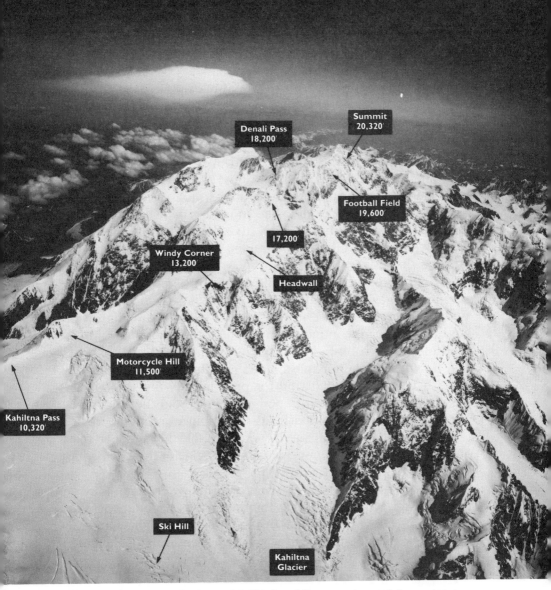

Summit
20,320'

Denali Pass
18,200'

Football Field
19,600'

17,200'

Windy Corner
13,200'

Headwall

Motorcycle Hill
11,500'

Kahiltna Pass
10,320'

Ski Hill

Kahiltna
Glacier

The West Buttress of Mount McKinley. **Map courtesy of Aeromap U.S.**

McKinley is queen of the vast Alaska Range, queen of the vast Alaskan Interior it commands. It is royalty, and its word is the law of this land.

"It's like a human," says Doug Geeting, one of the handful of bush pilots who make their living flying people to Mount Mc-Kinley during the prime spring and summer climbing season.

"You've got to treat it that way. If you treat it like a big rock, you won't last that long. It changes all the time. It's moody. It's never the same twice. It can be real nice and real warm, or it can just be a son-of-a-bitch."

Picturesque, dangerous, teasing, alluring, Mount McKinley beckons. It is high, it is icy, it is cold. Yet it is climbable. Some men fail, some men die. Others find a way. This is man at his best. He sees the insurmountable and surmounts it.

The Alaska Natives called the mountain Denali, "the Great One," or "the High One." The Natives knew that this monstrous bulk towering over all other mountains around it must be special, must be the only one of its kind.

In 1896 a prospector exploring Alaska's Interior came upon the mountain and gave it a new name. Marveling at its stateliness, William Dickey felt sure it must be the tallest mountain on the North American continent. He called the mountain Mount McKinley after soon-to-be President William McKinley. Dickey said he chose to honor the mountain with the Ohio politician's name because his nomination for president by the Republicans was the first news he heard upon emerging from the wilderness.

The next white men to visit the mountain were members of a United States Geological Survey team. In 1898 they mapped some of McKinley's lower slopes, including the glacier they named for the surveyor, Robert Muldrow.

In the years after these explorations, men were tantalized by the idea of climbing the highest mountain on the continent. Publicity about Dickey's find, about the immensity of this mountain in the distant wilderness, attracted the adventurers of the day.

Dr. Frederick Cook, who spent considerable time in the Arctic exploring with Robert E. Peary, made a circumnavigation of the mountain in 1903. In 1906 Cook returned to Mount McKinley and twelve days later emerged from the Interior claiming the first ascent of the peak. He wrote a book, published in 1908, to support his story. His claim was later discredited, however. In the following years it was proven that his summit photographs were actually taken on the Ruth Glacier, most assuredly in the proper neighborhood, but near the mountain's base, thousands of feet below the summit.

There were skeptics of Cook's claim long before his evidence was shown to be a hoax. In November 1909 a crudely equipped quartet of Alaskans sitting around a bar in Fairbanks scoffed at the reports they'd heard of Cook succeeding on McKinley. They figured no men were tougher than Alaskans, and they decided they would be the first men to stand on McKinley's summit.

The following April, they gave it a try. The climbers used a dog team to reach the 11,000-foot level on the Muldrow Glacier. Remarkably, after placing themselves in position, without ropes, with no climbing protection at all by modern standards, these men made a single-day attempt to reach the summit while carrying a huge wooden pole. They planned to plant the pole on the summit, where it would be seen by telescope from Fairbanks, nearly 150 miles to the north, then the most populated place in the region.

They began their assault at three A.M. on April 10, 1910, and over the course of one very long day, two of them, William Taylor and Pete Anderson, ascended 8,000 feet, finally reaching the summit of the north peak of Mount McKinley. To put this astounding feat in perspective, consider that today's guided climbing parties take about three weeks to climb McKinley. In all this time few people have ever matched or surpassed this accomplishment at high altitude.

Despite the brilliance of this climb, this was not the actual pioneer ascent of McKinley. Taylor and Anderson made a mistake. The real summit of McKinley is the south peak. The north peak is 19,470 feet above sea level and not the true summit.

The challenge of McKinley remained.

Mount McKinley was at last climbed in 1913. The four-member party was led by Hudson Stuck, the Episcopal archdeacon of the Yukon. But the first man to actually stand on the summit June 7, was Walter Harper, then twenty years old. Harper was a native Alaskan, half–Athabascan Indian and half-Irish. Harper was to survive McKinley's storms and whims on this climb, only to die a few years later at the age of twenty-five, when he and his wife drowned and sank with a capsized ship.

It was left to Stuck to write the story of the expedition that also put Alaska outdoorsman Harry Karstens and Stuck's young assistant, Robert Tatum, on the summit. His book was called *The Ascent of Denali.*

Stuck was a dispassionate and somewhat clinical describer of the sights he observed during the thirty-one-day assault of the mountain. "Our situation on the glacier floor," he wrote, "much of the time enveloped in dense mist, was damp and cold and gloomy. The cliffs around from time to time discharged their unstable snows in avalanches that threw clouds of snow almost across the wide glacier. Often we could see nothing, and the noise of the avalanches without the sight of them was at times a little alarming."

Stuck also reported that he had seen the pole left behind in the snow by the 1910 expedition, thus quieting the skeptics who didn't believe the sourdoughs had actually performed the climbing feat they claimed; the pole, after all, hadn't been visible from Fairbanks.

The Stuck climb established the route up McKinley. One approached via a long march from the north and ascended over the Muldrow Glacier. For decades, no other route was used up the slopes of the mountain.

Then, in 1951, Bradford Washburn, the distinguished director of the Boston Museum of Science, who had climbed McKinley via the Muldrow Glacier route first in 1942, and again in 1947 with his wife Barbara (the first woman to climb McKinley), pioneered the West Buttress route. This route begins on the Kahiltna Glacier.

Washburn, who is credited with most of the up-to-date mapping of the region, loved the mountain and its surroundings.

"It was my belief," he said, "that there is no more beautiful and magnificent, yet intricate and savage, spot on earth than the region immediately surrounding Mount McKinley."

Washburn's pioneer climb of the West Buttress was nearly as significant as the first ascent because it opened the mountain to the masses. It was the first time airplanes were used to put climbers in such an advantageous place to climb the mountain, saving them a miles-long trek over difficult terrain. Washburn's route has been taken by most of the recreational climbers who come to Alaska and hire professional guides.

In this era of the guided climb, when so-called citizen climbers flock to McKinley in spring and early summer the way they used to flood the more accessible national parks of the nation's flatlands, a thousand people seek to find their way to the top of McKinley each year. All but a small percentage of them climb the West Buttress. The West Buttress has been labeled with the misnomer "a walkup route" simply because it is less technical than other paths up the mountain.

Since Washburn's ascent, teams of climbers have found routes to the summit along the South Buttress, West Rib, and the Cassin Ridge, all of them more demanding than either the Muldrow Glacier or the West Buttress routes. Man is never satisfied: once he has succeeded in reaching the highest height, he seeks more difficult ways to reach that height.

None found a more difficult way than the 1967 climbing party of Art Davidson, "Pirate" Ray Genet, Dave Johnston, and five others. Not because of the ruggedness of terrain, but because of weather. They were the first winter ascent group.

In those days the number of climbers on McKinley was still measured by the handful, not the hundred, and no one, no one at all, had considered placing his body in the midst of howling, terrifying winter wind in the most desolate place in North America. Davidson recalls scrounging for climbers willing to make the attempt. Many men turned down the invitation to visit McKinley's inhospitable slopes in winter before the group was filled out.

Even today, top climbers who have mastered McKinley in the warmer seasons, and whose belts have notches from notable climbs in other parts of the world, shiver at the thought of McKinley's harshness in winter.

Geoff Radford, an Anchorage climber who has challenged large peaks in the Himalayas, is one of them. "Those guys had determination," he said of the original winter party. "It's a depressing time of year to climb. It's certainly a hardcore thing to do."

Todd Miner, another veteran McKinley climber, and a mountaineering instructor at the University of Alaska, Anchorage, feels the same way. "I'm not crazy enough to go up there in winter," he said.

And that is today, more than twenty years later, when climbing equipment has become more sophisticated.

The 1967 winter ascent group consisted of eight bold young men possessed of the same pioneering spirit of the 1910 Fairbanks sourdoughs. Davidson, then only twenty-two, sought to toughen himself in his training for the climb. He ran through the streets carrying snow in his bare hands. And he tested his will by sleeping outdoors in a thin tent in the minus-forty-degree winter temperatures of Fairbanks. It turned out that he needed all of the resilience, all of the resistance, all of the strength his body could muster merely to survive.

It was minus-thirty degrees on the Kahiltna Glacier when they made their initial camp, and it grew only colder, more brutal, more nasty, as they progressed.

The trip began badly. Only three days into the climb, while they were still on the glacier, one climber was lost. Jacques "Farine" Batkin fell into a crevasse and died.

The men persevered through perhaps the worst weather any man has ever faced—and faced down—anywhere in North America. Storms came and went, storms came and stayed. Wind pounded their ears with the ferocity of a crazed drummer. Wind and snow split the party, trapped each group, and convinced it that the others were dead. Yet they did not die, they lived and triumphed. Davidson, Johnston, and Genet reached the summit, becoming the first to ascend the mountain in winter. Their toes were frostbitten, and a helicopter flew the weakened men off the lower part of the mountain directly to the hospital, but they survived.

Davidson, now an Anchorage businessman, recounted the adventure of the climb in his book, *Minus 148*. The title hints at what McKinley can throw at man when it is in the worst of its moods. The figure represents the temperature—something on the order of minus-fifty—plus wind. The combined effect is off the bottom of the weather charts. In other words, colder than anything man had thought of before. That was McKinley at its worst during those days of February and March of 1967.

The men had been driven by a quest to conquer the unknown, the way Davidson explains it. After a lengthy period of recuperation and reflection, Davidson wrote his book. "No one had lived on North America's highest ridges in the winter twilight," Davidson wrote. "No one knew how long the temperatures would drop, or how penetrating the cold could be when the wind blew. For thousands of years McKinley's winter storms had raged by themselves."

This expedition showed that even at its nastiest, Mount McKinley could be beaten.

But not always. Later in the same year McKinley exacted retribution for this success, as if to say that man should not get too cocky, should not expect to climb and conquer all of the time. That summer seven men were killed on a single expedition, destroyed by a vicious storm. It was the most disastrous McKinley climb ever, and one of the worst mountaineering incidents in American climbing history.

And that was in the summer.

The next major accomplishment on the mountain was a summer ascent. In 1970, McKinley was climbed by a soloist for the first time.

Naomi Uemura, a famed Japanese adventurer who would figure prominently in inspiring Vernon Tejas's winter solo climb, made the ascent. Uemura had climbed 22,835-foot Aconcagua in Argentina, the Western Hemisphere's highest mountain, in fifteen hours; he was the first from his country to climb Mount Everest; and he later became the first man to drive a sled-dog team to the North Pole. He made the McKinley climb by himself in June, although there were other people on the mountain at the time.

Once a solo had been achieved, it naturally led the daring to think of a solo in winter.

Davidson wrote, "When we came down from the winter climb in 1967 we wondered when someone would be crazy enough to go back to McKinley in winter."

In 1981 a supremely strong and confident Alaskan adventurer, John Waterman, made the first serious solo attempt on McKinley in winter. Waterman failed. He disappeared on the climb, leaving behind only a brief, curious note implying that he knew he was on a suicidal mission.

Over the next several years, several ambitious climbers, some in groups, some alone, planned and carried out assaults on McKinley's slopes in the most extreme weather. Some climbers died, some were turned back by weather, some turned back when the daunting nature of the task was realized.

In winter 1983 a four-man group reached the summit of the West Rib, a difficult, exhausting climb that succeeded because of the overall strength and experience of the climbing party. It was the second team ascent of McKinley in winter. But the historic nature of the climb was overshadowed when it, too, ended in tragedy. Robert Frank, one of the quartet, tumbled to his death when he made a misstep on his descent. Once again, McKinley seemed to announce: Come if you dare, but be prepared to pay the price.

In February 1984, Uemura, then forty-four, returned with a new goal. A fresh challenge of McKinley—alone to the summit in winter—beckoned.

A national hero in his home country, emboldened by his successes worldwide, Uemura came back to the mountain once again seeking to achieve what no man had ever done. Given his résumé, his experience, his proven tenacity, it seemed no one was better prepared for such a task.

Demonstrating his boldness, Uemura traveled lightly, with not even a tent for shelter, and with no equipment to cook hot meals. He didn't plan to stay long on McKinley. Just go up in a businesslike way and descend swiftly. He marched out of Kahiltna Glacier base camp carrying two critical items he hoped would keep him alive. One was a seventeen-foot bamboo pole strapped around his waist for protection against crevasse danger; the other was forty pounds of caribou meat in a pack.

On February 12, two weeks after setting out into the virgin, blowing snows of McKinley on the West Buttress route, Uemura sent word by citizens band radio to a bush pilot that he had reached the summit. He placed a small Japanese flag there as testimony to the achievement and began his descent.

Uemura was on his way down, on his way home to safety. The weather turned on him, and abruptly he disappeared. Was he in a snow cave? Hunkered down under the snow for protection from the stunning winds and fresh storms? Had he slipped, a crampon catching an edge in an exposed position? Had he been caught in an avalanche?

When the sky cleared, bush pilots scoured the mountain from the air. A team of world-class climbers was flown in and they searched on the ground. No Uemura. No body. He had simply vanished.

Uemura had succeeded in climbing up Mount McKinley alone

in winter. But he had not finished the climb, he had not returned to tell the story of it. The mountain had bent but not truly yielded.

Four years after Uemura died, Vernon Tejas, a professional mountain guide living in Anchorage, set out to finish the job. With the spirit of Uemura filling his heart and mind, with a Japanese flag tucked into his pack, Tejas set off from Kahiltna Glacier in February 1988, on the West Buttress route, determined to be the first man to climb McKinley alone in winter and live.

The Route

There are several ways to climb Mount McKinley. Climbers can approach from several directions and follow different routes once they reach the mountain. The pioneer climbers trekked for miles from the north side and up the Muldrow Glacier. They would never have given much thought to approaching from the south because the city of Anchorage didn't even exist when the initial exploration took place. They came from Fairbanks.

The Muldrow Glacier is still a popular route for those who wish to make a traverse of the mountain, going up one side and down another. The Cassin Ridge approach to the summit is an extremely difficult route and attempted by only the most experienced of climbers. Likewise, the West Rib.

Tejas never hesitated in his choice. The only route he ever considered was the West Buttress.

"I know the West Buttress," he said. "Mountains are soloed by the easiest route first, then the harder ones. But the person doing even the easy route is breaking trail for everyone else."

It is like the story of the sparrow flying on an eagle's back, said Tejas. The sparrow flies higher than the eagle does, but the sparrow needs the eagle to get that high.

The West Buttress was not one of the pioneer routes explored or considered during the early part of the century, but it has evolved into the most popular and frequently climbed way to the summit. It is the route that the guide services use to take their clients to the top. About eighty-five percent of the 5,000-plus climbers who have now reached the summit of Mount McKinley have climbed the West Buttress route.

Although Tejas had climbed McKinley by other routes, the West Buttress was the one he knew best. He knew the location of every landmark, every hill, and every crevasse field. He knew the places to make camp, the places where the wind would be most fierce, the places that were steep, and the places that were flatter.

These things were so fixed in Tejas's mind because he had been up and down the route over a dozen times. He knew the West Buttress so well because in a sense it was his office, his place of business.

Here is an illustration of how much times have changed, of how the technology of mountain climbing and the sophistication of guiding services have brought the sport of mountaineering to the masses: So many citizen climbers have climbed Mount McKinley by the West Buttress route in recent years that among the hardiest of athletes and highly skilled mountaineers, it has come to be called a walkup route.

This is an exaggeration. There are numerous steep sections that require continual use of ropes and crampons, and the head wall rising from 14,000 feet is not a stretch to be taken lightly even by the world's best climbers. Still, the challenge of the West Buttress is not technical difficulty but weather. By the nature of its location, a few hundred miles south of the Arctic Circle and deep in the Alaska Range in the nation's coldest state, McKinley has always been regarded as a weather mountain. It is a weather mountain even in spring and summer, when sudden storms can blow in, mixing extreme temperatures with high winds and feet of fresh snow. It is most definitely a weather mountain in winter. Every minute in winter it is a weather mountain.

"Before Naomi, to solo in winter was almost unthinkable," said Tejas of the 1984 climb on which Japanese adventurer Naomi Uemura made the summit alone in winter but died on the descent. "It was no longer unthinkable. I had the psychological advantage. He did not."

Some of the best mountaineers in the world have come to McKinley thinking of it as a minor problem, only to be either stymied or slowed by its foul weather—in summer.

The current-day popularity of the West Buttress route could never have been foreseen by the men who first climbed it in the summer of 1951. That year represented the dawn of exploration of high mountains. It was in 1951 that Annapurna was climbed by a French expedition and became the first of the world's 26,000-foot mountains to be conquered. The Edmund Hillary–Tenzing Norgay conquest of Everest still lay in the future.

In 1951, when Dr. Bradford Washburn, the then-director of the Boston Museum of Science, organized his combination scientific and mountaineering expedition, he was told he was crazy. What little was known of the West Buttress indicated it was far too dangerous to climb.

Washburn remembers being warned that he would taint his reputation by tackling the West Buttress because he was doomed to failure.

"It's a shame you're going to do this because you've had such a record of success," a museum trustee told him. "You're going to fall flat on your face."

Washburn, however, had speculated that the West Buttress would be a shorter way to the summit. In 1947, Washburn had climbed McKinley by the Muldrow Glacier.

From this earlier reconnaissance, Washburn was certain the Muldrow Glacier was not the best way up McKinley. He had looked over from the summit, down to Denali Pass, and decided, "The West Buttress: It's a cinch." What would make the difference, what would make the West Buttress more accessible, he knew, was the airplane.

Washburn told anyone who would listen that there was no question in his mind that the West Buttress would be the shortest, safest way to climb McKinley. He had been there, he said, and he was convinced of it.

Washburn believed the West Buttress could be climbed by landing a small plane on the Kahiltna Glacier at 7,200 feet. The climber would have a head start to the top instead of having to hike through meadows and snows virtually from sea level up the Muldrow.

In June 1951, leading a team of eight, he set out to prove his case, but not without some trepidation, as he reported in the August 1953 issue of *National Geographic.*

"We were off on an adventure which already had my heart pounding with mixed feelings of excitement, and I must admit, a certain amount of apprehension," he wrote. "We were going to try what time after time had been declared impossible."

At that time, McKinley had been climbed only six times by any route, and Washburn had been part of two of the expeditions. He had not only been to the summit at 20,320 feet, but gone over it and down to just above Denali Pass at 18,200 feet. He had left a cache of scientific materials there.

Nowadays, there are Alaskan bush pilots who make nearly their entire living ferrying people back and forth to McKinley at the height of the climbing season, but in 1951 the small planes weren't as reliable and hadn't been used much in expeditions. When Washburn departed from Chelatna Lake, a hundred miles northwest of Anchorage, it was in a two-seater plane with Dr. Terris Moore as the pilot. Moore was the president of the University of Alaska in Fairbanks, and later wrote a book about the earliest climbs on Mount McKinley.

As the plane swooped out of the clouds, Washburn and Moore reconnoitered the Kahiltna Glacier, looking for a smooth spot to land. The view seemed to confirm the worst expectations of those who had warned Washburn not to go. It was bumpy and the ice surface was broken up. But after searching, they found a good spot and Moore set down. The plan was to leave Washburn and go back to get the others, one by one. When the plane lifted off and the drone of the engine evaporated, Washburn was alone on the glacier.

"It was so quiet I could hear my heart beat," he wrote.

Washburn pitched a tent and took a temperature reading. It was ten degrees above zero and the clouds were thickening, a portent of things to come. It only got worse. A full-fledged storm blew in. No planes would fly in this. Washburn was alone for two days before Moore could bring in any of his companions.

Once James E. Gale and Captain William D. Hackett had joined Washburn, they quickly trekked off the lower glacier and set up a base camp at 10,300 feet. These days, climbers use the original landing area on the Kahiltna as a base camp, but when the three men moved up past 10,000 feet for their prearranged supply air drop from the rescue squadron of the Alaska Air Command in Anchorage, they had advanced higher on the West Buttress than any man had gone. Their food drop included forty-eight loaves of bread.

McKinley continued to behave like an insecure child and hurled a new blizzard at them while they were still at 10,300 feet, pinning them down. When the weather cleared and they advanced above 13,000 feet, they encountered crevasses.

The climbers made a new camp and a new discovery: The wind could blow with hurricane velocity here. They called this place "Windy Corner."

On the Fourth of July the climbers awoke to a whiteout, a storm snarling at sixty miles per hour. It was then that one of the climbers uttered the incisive truth about Mount McKinley, a truth that every McKinley climber can identify with:

"This kind of climbing," said John Ambler, one of Washburn's partners, "is about ninety percent trying to stay alive and warm and only ten percent climbing."

Despite this inhospitable treatment by the mountain, Washburn said he and the others were "absolutely certain we were going to get up it."

The next day, July 5, the wind was blowing at eighty miles an hour and it was snowing, but the climbers were determined to move to higher ground. They climbed to 14,000 feet, and onto the head wall, then shoveled a trail in front of themselves up to 15,400 feet.

Feeling lethargic because of the altitude, the group slowed. Daunted by the steepness and snow, they tried to find another way higher by cutting through rocky ledges. They couldn't do it and instead cut steps for themselves in the snow.

More than thirty-five years later the memory of that labor remains vivid in Washburn's mind. He says he'll never forget those hours of chopping ice steps.

On July 9 the mountaineers were camped at the wide plateau at 17,200 feet, which today is the usual final camp for groups making a guided attempt for the summit.

A day later the sky was clear and they set out for Denali Pass. It was straightforward climbing with no surprises and no major obstacles. Shortly after noon, Washburn and the two others with him began to recognize contours and outcroppings. Washburn had been in this area before. And then he spied the cache he'd left behind four years earlier.

"I gave a shout of joy," he wrote.

The West Buttress route had been completed: He had already climbed down this far from the summit.

"We shook hands heartily," he wrote.

The climbers plodded on through the afternoon to the top on a beautiful summit day that offered views in every direction for over a hundred miles. They saw mountains, a very distant horizon, and mists shrouding Anchorage and Cook Inlet.

"Most impressive of all," Washburn wrote, "was the deep emerald green of the lowlands to the south and west . . . As Archdeacon Stuck said after his first ascent of McKinley thirty-eight years before, it was like looking out the very windows of heaven."

Washburn, Hackett, and Gale had reached the summit in only seven days from their 10,300-foot camp. Guided groups generally allow up to three weeks for an ascent from 7,200 feet. The other members of the Washburn team made the summit on July 13 and 14.

Washburn had been the first to arrive on the mountain and he was the first to leave. After his plane departed from McKinley and he left the white, frozen hillocks of the mountain behind, he was struck by the contrast with the land at sea level.

"The sun was slipping behind the vast Yukon lowlands to the northwest as we flew over Wonder Lake and glided into little Kantishna airfield," he wrote. "I'll never forget the lush green of that valley, the beauty of the spruces, and the smell of grass and flowers that came in the plane windows even before we touched the ground. The whole world down there seemed soft, fresh, and delicious after the cold, icy desolation of the heights."

The West Buttress route of Mount McKinley had been climbed for the first time.

Nearly forty years later, Washburn marveled that it had been climbed so frequently since, and shakes his head, tsk-tsking over the inexperience of some of those who try.

"If you stop all air support, it would not be the popular route it is today," he said. "The problems with the West Buttress today occur in two areas. People can climb McKinley with a two-week vacation and they go too fast. They get pulmonary or cerebral edema, or hypoxia. Or the weather."

Washburn was right. The West Buttress is a shorter way to the top. But it is not necessarily an easy way.

The Legacy of
Naomi Uemura

In the winter of 1984, Vernon Tejas was in Japan on a vacation, part of a year-long, around-the-world trip. He spoke little of the language, but gradually he became aware that the words "Mount McKinley" were being spoken on television newscasts, written in newspapers, and said aloud by average citizens.

Naomi Uemura, of Tokyo, a national hero for his adventures on mountains and for mushing sled dogs to the North Pole, had gone to Alaska for a winter climb of Mount McKinley. Uemura, fourteen years earlier, had become the first man to complete a solo ascent of North America's highest mountain. Now, at age forty-four, he was attempting to become the first to complete a solo ascent of McKinley in winter. No man had ever done that.

Uemura, a slightly built five-foot-four, had begun his climb in late January. He planned to dig snow caves for shelter and eat primarily frozen caribou meat and seal oil for nutrition. His was to be a lightning assault.

Once it became known that the famed Uemura was seeking

the prize of the first solo winter ascent, other top climbers assessed his chances with respect. "This is in no sense a foolhardy adventure," said Jim Wickwire, a Seattle mountaineer who was the first American to climb K-2, the world's second-highest mountain.

The first news that reached Japan was of Uemura's success. Braving temperatures of minus-thirty degrees to minus-fifty degrees Fahrenheit, he had made the summit on February 12 and let the world know via citizen's band radio. The Japanese were thrilled. Uemura, who had become a best-selling author by writing up the tales of his adventures, had become so well-known that his exploits were used in school textbooks as examples of bravery. The Japanese people believed they would soon be reading a new book about another triumph.

But the bad news followed quickly: Uemura had disappeared on McKinley.

Uemura was supposed to have returned to his base camp two or three days after leaving the summit. But there was no word from him. He was somewhere on the mountain. Rescuers were mobilized. Teams of park rangers, pilots, and distinguished climbers—some from Japan—rushed to the mountain to search for Uemura. Storms, too, rushed in, complicating the search and leading the rescuers to speculate that Uemura was either safe within a snow cave or lost in the great white vastness.

More than a week passed without a sign of Uemura except for the snowshoes he left behind at the base of the West Buttress headwall at 14,000 feet. By then, expert mountaineers had calculated, the fuel for his gas stove would have been exhausted. By then, they said, his cold food would have been devoured. The searchers, who had pledged to keep looking until they found Uemura or his body, were forced to quit without fulfilling either of those pledges.

Uemura remains somewhere on the perpetually frozen slopes of McKinley.

In Japan, Tejas witnessed the shift in the national mood from ecstasy to concern to mourning. Word spread among those he met that he was a climber, indeed was a climber who guided on Mount McKinley. People approached him. People asked him questions about the mountain. People sought him out to try to comprehend what Uemura had faced.

Tejas understood few of their words, but he could recognize "Uemura." And he could read the worry etched into the expressions of the Japanese citizens. Once, an older woman came up to Tejas. With tears streaming down her face, she spoke her countryman's name over and over: "Uemura, Uemura, Uemura." It would have been difficult indeed not to appreciate the depth of feeling surrounding the loss of this national figure.

Tejas was stunned that the intensity of their emotion toward Uemura led the Japanese to display their feelings so openly in front of him. People were overcome with sadness as they tried to talk to Tejas. They were frustrated by the language barrier. One man tried to converse for an hour, desperate to learn more of what might have become of Uemura.

"Ultimately," said Tejas, "there was just a real heavy silence." So many people were simply overcome by the power of what they felt for Uemura.

Tejas returned to Alaska and continued climbing and guiding clients on Mount McKinley for Genet Expeditions, the mountaineering company founded by Ray Genet. The experience of Uemura, and Tejas's own experience in Japan, though, planted a thought: Mount McKinley alone in the winter.

"I knew," said Tejas, "that it was indeed possible. The fact that Uemura didn't make it down meant that the journey was not yet finished."

Since 1984, Tejas had earned a reputation as a strong, methodical, cautious climber. Genet, who became a legend for climbing McKinley dozens of times before his 1979 death descending from the summit of Mount Everest, had been a flamboyant guide and believed that anyone who set foot on a mountain should climb to the top. Tejas felt otherwise. His philosophy was that one could always live to climb another day if the conditions were not right.

In his own, much quieter way, Tejas made a colorful statement. He was relentlessly upbeat. His head was shaved except for a wisp of a pony tail tied in back, and he had a thick and bushy dark beard. For sure, he did not blend in with the crowd physically. Yet Tejas was seen not as an eccentric climber, but as a reliable leader who didn't take unnecessary risks.

"He's always been a unique character to me," said Jim Hale, one of Tejas's early climbing partners, who is now a minister in

Talkeetna, the small Alaskan Interior town that is the staging area for most McKinley climbs. "I've always had tremendous respect for him. He's a very capable, careful, thoughtful person. I don't think I've ever seen him do anything foolish."

In the four years between Uemura's climb and his own, Tejas had enhanced his credentials in several ways. He had reached the summit of McKinley 12 times, he had been a member of the first winter team to ascend Mount Hunter, another difficult peak in the Alaska Range, and he had been a member of the all-Alaskan party that claimed the first winter ascent of Mount Logan in the Yukon Territory in 1986. Logan, at 19,850 feet, is North America's second-highest mountain.

Tejas had also performed a daring, near-solo rescue of two South Korean climbers just below McKinley's summit in 1986. The two Koreans would almost surely have perished if Tejas had not struggled through his own fatigue to haul them by rope up over the summit ridge to safety.

Gradually, as others tried and failed, Tejas came to realize that perhaps he had the strength, the will, to climb McKinley alone in winter.

"It was a flow of a decision," said Tejas. "Usually, I don't plan things very far in advance. It can be shattering when goals aren't met."

Uemura had died. John Waterman, another Alaskan and prominent climber, had disappeared on a winter solo. Then, in 1986, Dave Johnston, one of the members of the original winter ascent party, tried it alone.

Tejas was positive that Johnston would make it. A veteran climber, Johnston had already withstood the worst kind of weather that McKinley could hurl at a man. Johnston lives in a cabin close to the foot of McKinley, so he knew the territory better than almost anyone else. Tejas and Johnston talked it over, and Tejas felt Johnston's strength, competence and self-sufficiency in the wild would prevail. Tejas offered not only good wishes, but he lent Johnston some gear.

But Johnston didn't make it, either. He turned back with frost-bitten feet.

"I was giving him information and tools so that he could accomplish this," said Tejas, "and I started realizing that indeed it was possible for me to do the same."

All of the failures certainly made Tejas think twice, think many times, about whether it was worth a try. But what stuck in Tejas's mind was that Uemura had made it to the summit. He had not survived the whole journey, but he *had* made it to the summit.

"I know it's not going to be easy," said Tejas. "And if you look at the scorecard, it doesn't even look like it's smart."

Deep down, though, Tejas knew that climbers would keep assaulting McKinley, would keep trying, until someone made it. He figured other strong climbers in Alaska and even from the Lower Forty-Eight were probably considering the challenge. The attempts had received considerable publicity. Someone else was sure to take a crack at it, and in particular Tejas didn't like the idea of an Outsider coming in to claim the achievement.

As a man who made his living on Mount McKinley, as a man who had become as Alaskan as any who had come to the state, Tejas wanted to see an Alaskan perform this pioneer ascent.

"I wasn't planning on doing McKinley," he said, "but Naomi showed that it was within human capabilities, if you had a little luck on your side and knew what you were doing."

The way Tejas saw it, Uemura had already swiped the bragging rights for the first summer solo of McKinley and had nearly claimed them for the first winter solo, too. It was time for an Alaskan to reclaim the territory.

"This is our backyard. People are coming from around the world, coming here and doing things before we've done them," he said. "I think it's a little embarrassing not to be as familiar with our mountains as somebody from California or Japan, or anywhere. Why shouldn't we be the guys putting up the first ascents?"

Tejas was an Outsider once, but he had lived in Alaska for fifteen years and his soul belonged to the state. Alaskans have a reputation for being stubborn, proud, individualistic, and even eccentric. But above all, they have a reputation for being motivated and certainly possessive of their beautiful state.

"There is pride here, and I think it's well-focused pride," said Tejas.

By the time Tejas made his first tentative plans to climb McKinley alone in winter, he was seen as a man who knew the face of the mountain and its landmarks as well as he knew the trees and contours of his own neighborhood. In a sense, McKinley was Tejas's neighborhood.

One does not need a special permit to climb Mount McKinley. The National Park Service rangers who monitor traffic on the mountain do ask that climbers stop at the ranger cabin in downtown Talkeetna, register for their climb, and discuss their plans. Sometimes Chief Ranger Robert Seibert wishes he had the power of arrest to keep people with crazy plans and limited capabilities and experience from taking stupid risks, but he doesn't. Seibert can only try to talk them out of trying to do something that might kill them.

"We often attempt to modify people's plans," said Seibert, "but in the end the final decision is theirs. We get some pretty bizarre attempts. Soloing is one of them. We inform them of the risks. They say, 'I'll take that responsibility.'"

The rangers have no power to stop someone from climbing. If the power of persuasion fails, the climbers go. Sometimes the rangers have to rescue them. But of the thousand climbers who come from more than twenty countries each year to challenge McKinley, almost none of them do so in the winter. Seibert and the other rangers rarely have to talk someone out of trying a winter climb. The weather usually does it for them.

When Tejas called the rangers in February 1988 and dropped hints that he might make a winter climb in the coming weeks, they did not, as they ordinarily do, seek to discourage this climber. This time they were instead gripped by a sense of excitement; this time they believed that here was someone who knew what he was doing, someone about to attempt something historic.

"If anyone could make it," said Roger Robinson, a ranger who has climbed McKinley several times himself, "he could. He has so much experience on Denali. We see people who don't even know what climbing Denali's about. I get rather forceful at times to try to bring home to them how dangerous it can be."

Tejas was not running around Anchorage telling everyone he bumped into at the grocery store that he was going to climb

McKinley by himself in winter. He had first mentioned the idea to close friends the previous summer, but in fact, he told few people. He was a bit superstitious and secretive.

"I wasn't bragging, 'I'm going to do it,'" said Tejas.

Tejas spoke of the challenge again in Argentina in January, when he was guiding a climb of Aconcagua, the Western Hemisphere's highest peak. And he had told some people in Alaska. But he always qualified his statements. He told them he was planning to go, told them he might. There was always the chance that something would change, that something would come up and he wouldn't go.

Originally, Tejas considered simply going straight from Aconcagua to McKinley. That would have provided him with the optimum level of altitude acclimatization.

"I was totally loaded with oxygen," he said. "I was thinking, 'This would be the perfect time.'"

But when he returned home, two things slowed him down. For one thing, Tejas wanted to see how his girlfriend, Gail Irvine, reacted to the plan. He had just been away, climbing in South America, for two months, and he didn't want to ruin the relationship by immediately rushing off on another expedition. Climbing McKinley was not the first thing he mentioned to her when he got off the plane in Anchorage after returning from Argentina. He just didn't want to leave Gail so quickly.

Second, the bush pilot he felt closest to, the man he wanted to fly him to McKinley, was vacationing in Hawaii.

Pam Robinson, wife of Park Service Ranger Roger Robinson, works for Talkeetna Air Taxi. She was one of the first to know Tejas's intended timetable. She answered the phone when he called for pilot Lowell Thomas, Jr., son of the famous radio announcer.

"He very casually asked where Lowell was and when he'd be back, and he asked how much it would cost to fly to the mountain," said Robinson. "I asked him when he wanted to go. 'Right now,'" he said.

Tejas decided to wait until Thomas came back to Anchorage. It was important to Tejas to fly with Thomas. Although they work together professionally during the climbing season, their relationship transcends business. Tejas has a great deal of respect for

The solo winter ascent began with the help of trusted bush pilot Lowell Thomas, Jr., who flew Vernon Tejas to the McKinley base camp. Thomas was to return in sixteen days to pick the climber up, but the ascent didn't go according to plan. **Photo by Gail Irvine.**

Thomas's experience and opinions and he wanted to sound him out on the climb. Thomas, Tejas knew, was the pilot who received the citizens band radio call from Uemura in 1984 confirming his ascent to the summit.

Pam Robinson called Thomas in Hawaii, and he telephoned Tejas. He would support the plan.

"I thought, 'If anybody can do it, Vern can do it,'" said

Thomas. "I did think a little about how risky it would be. But I was very pleased he asked me to do the flying."

It was not only Thomas who backed Tejas during the final days of his preparation. Others who knew both the mountain and the mountaineer told Tejas to go for it. Seibert, Roger and Pam Robinson, and Charlie Sassara, a climber who was on the first ascent of the West Rib in 1983: all of them were pleased, not worried; thrilled for him, not discouraging.

"It was not only a vote of confidence, they were actually excited that I was going to try it," said Tejas. "I felt the excitement when I heard people saying, 'You really are the one to try it.'"

It made a difference. Talking only to himself, Tejas had had doubts. Talking to experts, he was reassured.

"These people not only knew me," Tejas said, "they knew the mountain, too, and they were still saying, 'You've got a chance; you're qualified.' And that had a lot of weight. I might think I'm capable of doing it, but unless other people believed in me, too, it was going to be a lot harder."

If he had a chance, Tejas finally decided, he would take the chance. He never viewed his winter assault on McKinley as more than a chance, never made a pledge, a promise, even to himself, that he would go for the summit at all costs. That would have been out of character for him anyway.

"I don't think I ever told anybody, 'I am going to climb it,'" said Tejas. "My idea was to take a shot at it. To try it. Even as I was leaving, I never said to myself that I was going to climb it. That was my desire, but given the tremendous variety of things that could go wrong—things that weren't going to work, the weather, the crevasses, the cold—I always said instead, 'I'll go as far as I feel comfortable going, give it a good shot.'"

What Tejas knew better than most was that the mountain would set the terms of the climb. If the mountain wanted to hold him back, it would hold him back. If the mountain wanted him to succeed, it would let him succeed.

One of the last things Tejas did before he left for McKinley was to pay his insurance premium.

Committed

Vernon Tejas sat in the car rubbing his hands together as his girlfriend, Gail, revved the engine to warm up the car. Usually for Tejas, the final moments before leaving on a major climb were frenzied ones. There was last-minute packing. There was the worry that something was being forgotten. But this time there was little of that. Tejas was organized. He had packed the night before, and even gotten some sleep.

It was about eight-thirty in the morning. The forecast for Anchorage that day called for clouds, temperatures in the twenties, and a chance of snow. There are about a hundred days between October and April when that forecast applies to Anchorage. Tejas didn't want that kind of weather. He wanted a clear day. A clear day meant good flying weather. A clear day meant that the climb could begin.

It was a ten-minute ride from the couple's South Anchorage home to Lake Hood, where famed bush pilot Lowell Thomas, Jr., parks his plane. In the car Tejas fidgeted and spoke little.

He was focused on what he was about to do, where he was about to go.

Gail was talking, and Tejas answered, "Yeah." Gail said something else and Tejas said, "Yeah." He was thinking. He had a transitory thought: "Am I doing the right thing?" Second thoughts, little doubts, crept into his mind. And then they were stilled. Tejas laughed at himself. *He couldn't get his hands warm.* Here he was, still in the city, in a car with the heater going, and he couldn't warm up.

"I haven't even gotten up there and my hands are cold," he thought. "If I'm cold *now,* what's going to happen *there*?"

There was Mount McKinley, 130 air miles north of Anchorage. The way in to Kahiltna Glacier at 7,200 feet, where Tejas would begin his trek to the summit of North America's tallest mountain in the middle of the harsh Alaska winter, was by small plane.

Less than three weeks before, Tejas had been in Argentina. He had spent January guiding and climbing on 22,835-foot Aconcagua. Though higher even than McKinley, it is not as difficult, and it is not a mountain that throws extreme weather conditions in the face of a climber. Nevertheless, for some people such a climb would be the expedition of a lifetime; for Tejas it was a training mission. Handling Aconcagua several times with ease meant he was fit, was ready for the toughest climb he had ever attempted. Aconcagua had definitely toughened him.

As he kissed Gail goodbye—a long kiss—he told her not to worry because he wouldn't do anything foolish. He told her he would be back soon. In two weeks, maybe sixteen days. In plenty of time to compete in the Iditabike, the mountain bike race from Knik to Skwentna and back, 210 miles across Alaska's Interior. In plenty of time for his thirty-fifth birthday, March 16. Heck, that was a month away.

At the hanger, Tejas and Thomas, a veteran McKinley pilot and former Alaskan politician who had once been lieutenant governor of the state, loaded the six-seat red-white-and-blue Helio-Courier prop plane. There was just enough room in it for the two men and Tejas's gear. The thing that made it so cramped was the ladder.

It had taken Tejas three years of off-and-on thinking and experimentation to settle on a common aluminum construction ladder as the key piece of equipment. That ladder was to keep Tejas alive.

The biggest problem, the biggest risk that solo climbers face on a snowbound, glaciated mountain like McKinley is crevasses. The yawning breaks in the ground can be covered only with thin layers of snow, and they fool even the most experienced, knowledgeable climbers into thinking their next step will be safe. Often, instead, they plummet into a cavernous hole and die. If a man roped to a partner falls into a crevasse, his fall may be arrested by the tightening line, and he is frequently rescued by the strength of his partners. He may survive with only a scare. A climber traversing a crevasse field alone is in far greater peril. He may survive the fall into the hole, but likely will face a severe problem climbing out. He may perish not from injuries but from exposure or starvation, and his body may never be found.

Uemura had used bamboo poles to protect himself. Other climbers doing solo climbs have constructed their own safety devices. The essential elements of these protective devices are twofold: they have to be light enough to be carried without inhibiting the climber's maneuverability; and they have to be long enough to span a wide crevasse if the climber stumbles into one. Tejas had thought long and hard on the problem. He had tested polevault poles, bamboo poles, and a complicated harness system. Then he went out to the Fred Meyer store and for about $75 bought a sixteen-foot, eighteen-pound aluminum extension ladder that came in two sections. He would wear it while traversing crevasse fields, where it might well save his life. He could also lash the sled with his gear to it and pull it along.

Tejas had to be sure the ladder was strong enough to hold his weight. While still in the store, he put the ladder up on two milk crates and jumped on it. It bent. His eyes went wide.

"It was real sobering," he said. "This ladder has to be able to save my life."

Not without some modification, it wouldn't. Tejas bought the ladder. But he reinforced it and fitted the two sections together so that they were doubly tough in the middle, turning the ladder into a thicker, twelve-foot-long lifeline.

There was no crowd at Lake Hood to see Tejas off. He had approached his challenge with an absolute minimum of fanfare.

34

What at first appears to be an odd (yet oddly appropriate) piece of gear for a climber was Vern Tejas's protection against falling into a crevasse. Worn around the waist, the ladder is intended to straddle glacial cracks. **Photo by Lowell Thomas, Jr.**

He had made no announcements to the media. Perhaps fifteen people knew he was embarking on the climb. The Denali National Park rangers—Bob Seibert and Roger Robinson—had encouraged him. He worked with those guys all summer. In a sense, they were the custodians of the mountain, the men who helped the guides, the men who tried to dissuade the foolish and unprepared from setting foot on McKinley. They hadn't tried to dissuade Tejas. He was neither foolish nor unprepared. He had been on McKinley fourteen times, and he knew the West Buttress route as intimately as any man alive.

No, there was no reason to tell the world he was going for a walk in the snow. Word would get out anyway, Tejas was sure. Tejas was a man who believed in letting actions speak for themselves. He disliked braggadocio and was even less motivated to advertise a failure in advance, if that was what it was to be. There were no guarantees. Other brave, strong men had failed to best the mountain. Tejas thought he could do it, thought he was as prepared as a human being could be to climb McKinley in winter. He wouldn't be here in an airplane if he wasn't. But Uemura must have felt the same way, must have been convinced of his readiness, must have known how few were as strong, as experienced. And Uemura, Tejas reminded himself, never came down from the mountain.

Tejas and Thomas, old friends who well understood the monumental task Tejas had chosen and the dangers he faced, spoke little during the hour-plus flight from Anchorage, over the Matanuska-Susitna Valley, into the Alaska Range, to McKinley. The day was clearer than promised.

They discussed the ladder. Tejas told Thomas he had a Japanese flag with him and would plant it on the summit as a gesture of respect to Uemura. Thomas said he thought that was an honorable thing to do.

Tejas, about to embrace a mission of solitude, was already being borne away by private thoughts. Mostly they were about what everyone would think if he didn't reach the summit, if he changed his mind and turned back.

"Who am I letting down?" he thought. "Myself, of course, but I can live with that." The inevitable thought filtered in. "If I turn back, what will people think?" Sometimes it's harder to live with letting other people down.

Tejas didn't want to let down Gail, his friends, other climbers, or Thomas. These were the people who cared the most about him. The closer people were to him, the more Tejas felt they had invested in him, the more he wanted to do it for them, to pull off this impossible dream of a climb.

Then he remembered one of the last things Gail had said to him before he left: "You can always turn around. At any point you want to. At any time."

As the plane approached the mountain, its hugeness as always intimidating, even to men like Tejas and Thomas who know it, explore it, experience it every summer, Thomas was struck by the pristine nature of the snow. In summer, with pilots flying in and out, climbers tromping all over the place, the Kahiltna Glacier is transformed into a miniairport. It had been months since a man had walked here, though. The snow was smooth and fresh, unmarked.

"It looked like no one had ever been there," said Thomas.

Thomas landed comfortably at about eleven A.M. It took about a half hour to unload the plane. Then they stood there, a bit awkwardly, trying to make their separation one of their routine partings before a routine summer guided climb.

"So long. Have a good climb," said Thomas.

Thomas stepped back into the plane, taxied down the glacier, and lifted off. For several moments Tejas could hear the buzzing of the engine. And then he heard nothing but the sound of his footsteps crunching on the snow.

It was then that the magnitude of it all settled on Tejas. The rush of preparations, the uncertainty of the weather, the flying, the unpacking—all the details had occupied him for days. Now it was him and the mountain. No one else, nothing else.

Tejas looked around at the great whiteness all around him.

"*Big* country," he thought. "What am I doing here? I'm committed now. He's not gonna be back for two weeks, no matter what."

Unexpected Company

For four hours, Tejas worked with his gear, organizing the sled he would pull behind him when he began walking, and organizing his mind, preparing mentally to start up the mountain. It was peaceful being alone on the Kahiltna Glacier.

And then a familiar sound pierced the silence, faintly at first, then louder. It came closer. It was the sound of an airplane engine.

What's this? Tejas thought to himself. What plane could possibly be flying in the middle of winter? It wouldn't be a sightseer. It wouldn't be Thomas, who had no reason to return. The plane swooped down from the clouds and landed on the glacier, close to where he stood.

Tejas was stunned.

"I am getting psyched," he said. "Here I am, definitely alone, and then here comes the plane."

Another small plane. Carrying a climber. Another climber with the intention of soloing Mount McKinley in the winter.

And not just any climber, either. The climber was a man Tejas had met in Argentina barely a month before, a strong climber who was a member of the group he had guided to the summit of Aconcagua. Tejas and the other man had had disagreements on the climb. As always a cautious leader on a guided trip, Tejas had attempted to slow the pace of the group because of bad weather.

This other climber, Geoffrey Lyon, a Californian, had apparently mistaken his safety-first approach as a sign of weakness and had protested. As a result, the two men were not on the friendliest of terms. Now here was Lyon again, butting in on Tejas's party. It was too bizarre. Since when had two climbers in a single year attempted McKinley solo in the winter, never mind two climbers at the same time?

"The *same day,*" said Tejas.

If Tejas had attempted to coordinate simultaneous arrivals on the glacier with a friend back in Anchorage, he doubted it would have worked out. Something would surely have intervened to mess up the plan.

It was not that Tejas had no inkling that something like this could occur. When he had registered with the McKinley rangers, they told him another climber had made inquiries about a solo winter attempt. But he didn't expect anyone to try at the same time, and certainly not someone he knew.

Tejas was upset about Lyon's arrival, not only because it was Lyon, someone he had tangled with recently, but because he had no one to blame for Lyon's presence but himself. While he was in Argentina, he had let slip his intention to climb McKinley alone in the winter. Tejas knew Lyon got the idea from him.

Aconcagua had been Tejas's testing ground for this climb, his final proving ground for himself. He had gone to South America in December and ridden a mountain bike days on end at altitudes ranging from 5,000 to 17,000 feet.

He reached Aconcagua, the monster peak of the South American continent, in January. Aconcagua is not a technically difficult mountain to climb. The snow line can be as low as 14,000 feet, or as high as 18,000 feet. In an isolated, southern portion of the country, a half-day's bus ride from Mendoza, the nearest big city, the mountain area is very dry, and the main climbing route has a great deal of talus and crushed rock. Aconcagua is known as a walkup, especially for a world-class climber. Its attractions are its height and its distinguishing characteristic of being the tallest mountain on the continent. Altitude and the potential for stormy weather, including high winds, are the obstacles facing climbers on Aconcagua. For seventeen days Tejas led a guided climb of the peak. There were five people in the group, including Lyon.

Little did Tejas realize when he escorted the group out of the mountains to a nearby community and saw them off that he would meet Lyon again soon. His thoughts were far from any such encounter. At that time he was eager to return to Aconcagua and further test and improve his fitness.

Tejas went back to Aconcagua planning to perform one of the world's more peculiar sporting feats: he would take his mountain bike up the mountain and then turn around and ride it down.

Half stunt, half endurance test: Vern Tejas pushed his mountain bike up the slopes of Aconcagua, the highest peak of the Western Hemisphere, just weeks before challenging McKinley in winter. **Photo courtesy of Vernon Tejas.**

Tejas had brought the sturdy bike with him from the United States. He'd shipped it to the home of Phillip Hansel II, a brother two years younger, who lived in New Orleans, and tested it in a race in that city.

When it comes to Aconcagua, though, "riding a bike" means something different from the commonly accepted sense of the words. It wasn't as if Tejas pedaled along flat ground. There was no flat ground. But he did ride a portion of the way up to 14,000 feet. After that the terrain compelled him to dismount. He came to a river crossing and lashed the bike on his back. Sometimes he pushed the bike. Other times he pulled it. The last 1,000 feet to the summit involved scrambling on a moving rock field. For a little while every step he took forward carried Tejas two steps backward.

It was when he finished that crazy ascent of Aconcagua that Tejas knew he had the fitness to tackle McKinley.

"Everything I was doing was working out," said Tejas.

Not only had he climbed Aconcagua a second time, he had hauled a bicycle up there with him. He ascended 8,000 feet in a single day. That was moving and Tejas knew it. It built confidence as well as endurance, and it made him think that yes, he was getting pretty tough, and yes, a solo ascent of McKinley in winter could become reality.

Tejas may have been seeing reality; the next day other people on the mountain probably thought they were seeing an apparition. Tejas was descending from 22,835 feet to base camp at 14,000 feet on his mountain bike. They saw a powerfully built man wearing goggles, a red crash helmet, and red snow suit, with a thick beard and a thin pony tail flapping behind, careening wildly down the mountain. The man would ride the bike a few yards, crash into a rock, tip over, right the bike, and start again. And then he hit the true trails. The bike picked up speed and he rode that thing like a bucking bronco, twisting and turning.

When Tejas reached bottom, exhilarated, he posed for pictures for gaping, cheering climbers, then parked the bike and prepared to climb Aconcagua a third time, this time carrying a parasail. He climbed to 20,000 feet and spent the night, and then the next morning as the clouds dissolved and the Andes spread before him, he climbed to 22,000 feet. Then he *jumped off the mountain.*

For twenty minutes he was a soaring bird, gliding off the face of the huge rocky mass, cruising through the thin air four miles above sea level, down, down, down, to base camp again.

Tejas knew then he was strong enough for anything.

On McKinley, on the Kahiltna Glacier, as Lyon unloaded, Tejas kicked himself. He had told so few of his own friends about his plan to solo McKinley and yet he had let out his plans to a near-stranger too casually in the euphoria of his triumphs at Aconcagua.

Still, one does not make enemies on big mountains. Having friends can mean having someone around to save your life, if it becomes necessary.

Tejas ambled over to Lyon and the man who flew him in, bush pilot Cliff Hudson, and offered to help unload the plane. Tejas studied Lyon's gear, wondering if the Californian had brought what he needed, wondering if he would be safe. Tejas, who had so much experience on McKinley, worried briefly that he might have to choose between going ahead with his own climb and rescuing Lyon, who had no experience on McKinley. He knew what he would do: the climber's obligation is always to rescue a fellow climber in danger. He just didn't want the situation to come to that.

It was four P.M. Tejas had intended to spend the night on the glacier, but the arrival of Lyon altered his plans. He didn't want the guy breaking trail for him. A solo was a solo. That meant you did it yourself.

The Race Is On

Tejas moved for the sake of moving. With daylight rapidly dwindling, he knew he wouldn't go far that first night. He hiked perhaps a mile on the Kahiltna Glacier and made camp.

For Tejas, making camp meant digging a snow trench, taking a shovel from his sled, and digging into the thick snow. He did not even carry a tent up the mountain with him.

In theory, a tent sounds like a prudent investment, but the theory falls apart in hellacious weather. A snow shelter is warmer and more reliable in high winds.

Tejas had learned that from experience. The flaps on a tent can bang all night long, interrupting sleep. (When he does bring a tent on a climb, Tejas also carries ear plugs.) High winds can even blow a tent away. Then there's blowing snow to contend with. A climber can be up half the night digging out a repeatedly buried tent. No, Tejas had taken a lesson from the Eskimos. The Native people of the Arctic didn't use tents, they built igloos. These shelters are insulated and quiet, and they don't blow away.

43

People may look askance at a house of snow, and by indoor housing standards, it can be cold. At no time in one of Tejas's snow shelters did the temperature get higher than freezing, but it was twenty below zero outside at the time. Even in temperatures as low as the twenties above zero, a man can briefly expose his hands for necessary tasks.

Tejas had brought a tent as far as base camp, but he had left it there. Tejas preferred to rely on his own skills at digging trenches, cutting snow blocks, and constructing shelters out of the materials at hand. A tent was extra weight, and he was already hauling about 150 pounds of gear. Many people consider a tent to be the most rudimentary piece of equipment, the most critical tool, for an extended stay in the outdoors, but Tejas had learned how to make the snow, with its natural insulating qualities, work to keep him warm.

Tejas had invested years in perfecting his snow shelters. A friend with the Alaska Mountain Rescue Group, named Udo Fischer, was an illustrator who had written and drawn a pamphlet on arctic survival. Reading the pamphlet gave Tejas his initial vision for a snow shelter, but he developed his own version. Before their 1986 winter ascent of Mount Logan in the Yukon Territory, he and the other climbers went to a wilderness area about fifty miles from Anchorage and spent a day doing nothing but digging trenches.

Tejas had also studied the techniques of Air Force survival experts. He didn't just attack a pile of snow willy-nilly and try to shape it into something.

These are not snow houses with multiple stories and awnings. These are basic survival shelters. An hour of digging produces a trench shelter that is perhaps eight feet long, three feet wide at the shoulders, and four feet deep. All in all, about the size of a living room sofa. Tejas places his skis and poles across the trench, then lays his survival ladder on top of them, followed by a tarp. On McKinley, the tarp he used was his sky-diving parafoil. (Shades of Aconcagua.) In fact, Tejas secretly hoped to use the parafoil for a flying descent off the mountain. Weather permitting, of course.

If the wind is blowing when he is building such a trench (which

Tents must be carried; tents can be blown apart by vicious winds. So Tejas dug snow shelters on McKinley. Bricks of snow wall in this shallow trench, which is ready for its parafoil roofing. **Photo by Vernon Tejas.**

it usually is on McKinley), Tejas also constructs a two-foot-high wall of snow blocks to deflect the gusts.

"I know *how* to shovel," said Tejas. "I have the muscles for it, and the aptitude for it, if there is such a thing." Indeed. Tejas spent one winter supporting himself as a snow shoveler in the small Southcentral Alaska community of Valdez, where the Trans-Alaska Pipeline ends. In Valdez they measure snow in feet, not inches.

"I actually enjoy building these shelters. I've practiced building them. I've refined them and defined them. I've picked up tips from several other experts. In my opinion, it's just a better way to go."

45

The more he dug, the better he got. Tejas became increasingly proficient at building the survival shelters while on McKinley, so proficient that by the time he came off the mountain, it was taking him only an hour between the time he dropped his pack to make camp to the time he crawled into his sleeping bag.

"I got it wired on McKinley," he said. "I had twenty-nine days to practice."

As Tejas dug, Lyon skied up to him and thanked him for breaking trail. He watched Tejas's labor with interest, asked what he was doing, and eventually settled into his own camp a few hundred yards farther on. He had a tent.

Although he was unhappy to have company on the mountain, Tejas resolved to be polite to Lyon. They exchanged pleasantries and small talk. It would have been ludicrous to be camped just down the trail from one another, the only human beings in this desolate spot, and try to pretend the other didn't exist, Tejas reasoned.

When climbers land at the airstrip on the Kahiltna Glacier, they are at 7,200 feet on the 20,320-foot mountain. Base camp is in a flat area on the southeast fork of the glacier, surrounded by the spires of beautiful mountains in the Alaska Range. If it is clear, climbers can see Mount Foraker, Mount Hunter, and even the rising bulk of McKinley itself. As they head for the beginnings of the West Buttress route, climbers go down Heartbreak Hill and drop in elevation to about 6,800 feet onto the main glacier before the trail rises again.

Heartbreak Hill is not named after the stretch of hills in the Boston Marathon known by the same name. McKinley has its own heartbreaks. As you come down the mountain, returning to base camp, it is the final, tiring uphill area about two miles from the end of the trip. Tejas said he first described the terrain as Heartbreak Hill when he was guiding a group of Boy Scouts in 1982. The name became common usage for the area in the following years.

The second day out, Tejas advanced a few miles. He decided to lessen his burden by splitting his gear into two bundles. This meant he had to cover the same ground twice to bring everything forward. Lyon, who was carrying fewer supplies, carried his gear all at once and moved ahead of him—Tejas presumed only a short way—out of view. When he went to sleep that night, Tejas did not know exactly where Lyon was.

When Tejas awoke on the morning of February 18, he knew this snow cave would be his home for a while. Climbers on big mountains learn to read weather. They gauge wind strength and study clouds. Sometimes the signs are subtle and sometimes they are as blunt as a punch in the nose. This morning the wind was roaring and Tejas knew it would be folly to try to fight it.

The wind blew all that day and all the next. Hard and howling. A man in a tent might spend his time fearful that his shelter would be uprooted and carried away on the wind. A man underground would be snug, out of danger, if he had built his shelter well.

There is always the danger of asphyxiation in a snow trench. The carbon monoxide lingers from the cooking stove. Even if a climber does a good job of putting in chimneys, high winds can drift snow over their tops and block them. More than once on the trip, Tejas awoke in a panic, his breathing restricted. He kept a ski pole by his sleeping bag, ready to poke holes in a blocked chimney.

"Several nights I woke up gasping," he said. "It felt like I was locked in a freezer. I got claustrophobic."

When the wind blows on Mount McKinley, it is of a type that does more than rattle windows. It turns conversation into shouting matches. It gives people headaches. It keeps climbers pinned inside their tents awake at night. They go home talking of being driven nearly mad by the constant roar.

A few feet under the ground, cushioned by the snow, Tejas was away from the brunt of this. He was hardly weary from his exertions only a few days into the journey, but ever-methodical, ever-cautious, he focused on keeping both his water bottles and his belly full as he lay stuck in the snow.

It's easy to suggest sleeping in as long as there is time and the knowledge that the energy will be needed later, but that never really worked for Tejas. He woke up at six-thirty or seven in the morning anyway, and faced long days with nothing much to do. He couldn't stand up in the snow shelter, so he developed a half-hour workout routine to keep his muscles toned up. He did push-ups, situps, leg raises, and stomach raises while lying on top of his sleeping bag.

"You don't know if you're going to be there for a week," said Tejas. "Stretching is important if you're going to lay around in your bag all day. One of the problems that afflicts mountaineers on a climb is poor circulation. You can get frostbit in the bag."

For entertainment Tejas listened to the radio. In late afternoon he turned the dial to KSKA-FM, the Alaska Public Radio station out of Anchorage. He lay there listening to "All Things Considered" and, later, "Alaska News Nightly."

At other times, Tejas, who is as intensely interested in music as he is in climbing, made his own music. He played the harmonica for hours. He got more practice in a few days than he'd had all year.

After two days, though, Tejas was out of songs and, to some extent, out of patience. He wanted to move. He was eager to make progress, and he wondered about Lyon.

The fifth day on the mountain, February 20, saw the wind die down enough for Tejas to break out of his shelter and begin moving higher up the mountain. It was good to be out and going again, though progress was comparatively slow. The Kahiltna Glacier is heavily crevassed. There have been many accidents, many deaths on this part of the mountain, some resulting from the overconfidence of climbers. This was a critical area for Tejas and his reliance on his aluminum ladder. Tejas moved slowly. He would be happy if he never had to test its strength.

At the end of a good climbing day he reached the base of Ski Hill, an incline that rises off the glacier. Though steep, it is not especially onerous to climb because steps can be kicked into the snow. Ordinarily, when Tejas guides groups on the mountain, they reach the bottom of Ski Hill, roughly 7,800 feet, in a single day from base camp. But that speed comes from the theory of safety in numbers. The climbers are roped together and provide mutual protection against disaster.

Between the necessity to travel extra carefully and the lost days, it had taken Tejas five days to reach this point. He had planned on a sixteen-day climb. Already he was behind schedule.

Tejas and Lyon had drawn even once again. Still figuring it was silly to pretend they weren't near one another, Tejas built his camp within voice range of Lyon's. They exchanged a few words before bedding down.

That night, back under the snow, Tejas felt good. He might have been moving slowly, but at least he was moving again.

The next morning, February 21, Tejas was up early and ready to go before Lyon had finished packing his gear. Lyon had apparently decided that snow shelters must be the right way to go and left his tent and stuff sack at the campsite.

That day both men assaulted the slope of Ski Hill. Tejas stuck to his double-hauling plan, making duplicate trips over the same terrain. When he dug his newest snow home that night, Tejas was camped at about 9,200 feet. Lyon—and this would prove important in the coming days to Tejas's peace of mind—had gone farther along the trail, camping somewhere near 10,000 feet.

The winds arrived again in the middle of the night. As soon as he woke up, Tejas knew he would not be climbing that day. The winds were loud and furious once more and they whipped snowflakes into the frenzy of a disturbed hive of bees. Trapped again. Another long day underground, waiting. The next day, February 23, dawned the same way. More wind. More snow. Tejas had not counted on this. The heaviest snows of the year on McKinley come in summer, when the weather warms up. In the winter, when the air is so frigid it is almost a tangible, brittle thing, it generally snows less. Winter brings the cold, but it is often accompanied by stillness. The temperature, as Tejas lay once more in his own hive of sorts, was minus-ten degrees. Most places on earth, that would be considered extreme cold. On McKinley, it was a heat wave.

The stormy weather presented problems. It played havoc with Tejas's schedule. His game plan allowed for no more than four storm days limiting travel on the mountain. But he'd already used them up.

At this rate, not only would it take him much longer to reach the summit and get home than he'd expected, but he'd also run out of food. Tejas made his first strategy change, a concession to the weather. He put himself on half rations for as long as he was pinned down. As a veteran McKinley climber, and as a guide who knew the mountain's nooks and crannies, Tejas knew that caches of food were often left behind by groups anxious to abandon the mountain swiftly after reaching the summit. This was against park service rules, but it was done. If he needed to replenish his supplies, he believed, he would be able to find a snowbound cache of food at one of the commonly used camps higher on the mountain.

During the second day of that storm, Tejas made an attempt to contact the outside world by using a lightweight citizens band radio. As always while climbing, he carried the batteries in his pocket to keep them warm and ready to go. Now he inserted them and tried two call-outs on this day. Wary of wasting the batteries, he stayed on the radio for just thirty minutes, hoping for any kind of response. But no one heard him. He left the radio monitor on for a little while longer, then gave up. Probably no one would be able to hear him until he got higher, he thought. Probably not until he reached 14,000 feet.

By the third day of the windstorm, Tejas was itchy to move. He climbed out of the snow shelter and found himself standing in a whiteout. Snow was blowing in his face and visibility was limited to a few feet. If he had been on the mountain in his job as a guide, with responsibility for the safety and lives of perhaps a dozen people, many of them comparative novices, Tejas would never have moved out of camp that day. But he was by himself, accountable to no one else, and he decided to take a chance.

There is a tremendous difference in a climber's mind-set when he begins his day with a clear sky, bright sun, and unlimited visibility, than when he is heading out into a storm that can slow him, throw him off the trail, and wipe out his field of vision.

Calm days provide a psychological lift for a climber. Stillness means comfort. When the sun is out, it's warming not only physically, but mentally as well. As Tejas puts it, climbers make tracks in nice weather. But being in a whiteout distorts everything. To advance at all, a climber must stick his ski pole in front of his feet to test the firmness of the cover, and he must stop frequently to check his compass. Moving more than a handful of steps at a time can be hazardous. The entire process is extremely laborious.

Two things played important roles in Tejas's choice to move. For one thing, he knew this mountain: knew it at its best, knew it at its worst, knew its twists and turns. He thought he understood what it was capable of. He did not underestimate that. But he had been past this point, what, thirty times? Up and down, on climbs and rescues at least that many. For another, the wind had shifted behind him. Certainly it blew strongly, but it would give him a tailwind, perhaps push him along a bit; maybe this storm was localized and the wind would help him climb above it.

Wind that comes over Kahiltna Pass often brings nasty business with it. The pass is a wind tunnel and usually climbers try not to linger just below.

"Visibility is zero-zero. That particular place on the mountain catches hell," said Tejas.

He figured if he could get beyond it, he could outrun the wind around a corner. That, too, he knew from past experience. It was worth a try, he thought.

Tejas set out, hooked to his sled, wearing his ladder, compass in hand. He could see nothing beyond the end of the ladder six feet in front of him. Nothing but white. Snow. Clouds.

"White on white on white," he said. "You can't tell if the snow is going up, or down, or what."

As he walked, he tossed three-foot bamboo wands with the thickness of a pencil, each tagged with brightly colored surveyor's tape, into the snow in front of him. The wands helped provide him with the depth perception he needed in order to know whether he was going to walk into a crevasse. Sometimes they sank out of sight. Better the wands than the climber.

"A couple of times they did save my bacon," said Tejas.

The temperature was about ten below zero. The wind blew at perhaps thirty miles an hour. On exposed skin, that would feel like fifty below zero. Fifty below zero is painful, and any kind of prolonged exposure can mean disaster.

Tejas would inch ahead about twenty steps at a time, then stop and take a reading on his compass. He feared walking off the edge of the mountain. Twenty steps, stop and read. Twenty steps, stop and read. For four hours. Baby step after baby step. He made it past 10,000 feet, past Kahiltna Pass, and stopped at a basin at 11,000 feet that was a natural camping spot. He wasn't out of the storm, but he did know where he was.

Tejas saw no evidence of his competitor and didn't know whether Lyon had climbed higher on the mountain or was himself burrowed under the snow. For days Tejas would fret about Lyon. Tejas had set out to be the first man to solo McKinley in the winter. He wasn't interested in risking his life to be the second.

He tried not to let thoughts of Lyon preoccupy him. He had other things to worry about, but Lyon was always in the back of his mind, nagging at him, making him wonder. Sometimes Tejas thought, "Wow, all this could be for coming in second place." And that didn't make him feel good at all.

"I didn't want to put out that much energy and time and effort and risk to be second best. The problem was that I had gotten the guy started on this climb myself, that I had caused my own problems. It made it a lot more interesting."

Tejas said he actually thought of himself and Lyon as characters in a novel. It was the kind of plot complication a writer of fiction would create for drama's sake. It was a weird situation. Not knowing whether Lyon, whom he knew to be a strong climber, was plodding on ahead of him discouraged Tejas, and once or twice the uncertainty teased him into considering quitting.

"I almost backed down," he said. "I almost decided not to go on. Then I thought, 'Why should I let this guy have that much power over my life?' I just said, 'No, I'm going to do it anyway, and if he does make the top, I'm still going up there, just for me.'"

What Tejas had no way of knowing was that Lyon was not ahead of him, not ahead of the wind. No. Lyon, still trying to master the complexities of constructing snow trenches, did not venture out on February 24 at all, the day Tejas braved the storm. Lyon was inside, suffering the beginnings of frostbite on his toes. Tejas probably passed within feet of him, but never knew it.

Tejas, not knowing whether he was chasing a shadow or a man, sat in his snow trench wondering.

Solitude

Climbing big mountains alone can be both a lonely and a dangerous occupation. If one stumbles, trips, sprains an ankle, or loses his way, death can beckon. There is nobody to send for help. There is nobody to hear cries for help. One misstep and a man can watch himself die, feel the life ooze out of his body as he awaits a rescue that will never come.

A solo climber must be totally self-sufficient and he must be aware at all times that he is fending for himself. When he's alone on a big mountain, every step is a dangerous step. When he's alone on a big mountain in winter, the danger is magnified and multiplied.

To those who do not have a feel for the sport, do not understand its rewards, the reasons for soloing a big mountain can be as difficult to explain as love. What passes between two lovers is their secret, their private communication. The rest of the world is excluded.

It is the same for those who solo big mountains. What passes between the man and the mountain is their private communication. The rest of the world is out there, beyond them. Solo mountain climbing offers the privacy of being the only human being, the last man on earth. The man who succeeds must face that lonely privacy, must cope with the fear and suppress it as he challenges the mountain. He must be content to be that last man.

Reinhold Messner, the great conquerer of all the world's highest peaks, has spoken of the intense feeling of aloneness that a solo climber faces. He likens it to looking into "a dizzy void."

Men who seek glimpses of the dizzy void seek glimpses of their own souls. Noise of cities, sounds of daily life, voices of friends are left behind. Only the business of exploring self remains.

When Tejas climbed to this camp at about 11,000 feet, he thought he was camping for the night. But no. McKinley, in its winter rage, delivered new storms, storms with frightening power. The snow trench he dug that day became the new prison, though a comparatively pleasant one—minimum security. At this place on the mountain, the hillocks provide protection from the furious wind. They deflect it and even block its howl.

Inside, in the snow and out of the danger, Tejas was hunkered down in quiet at six-thirty in the morning on February 26. He could turn on his little transistor radio with its headphones—a great $20 investment—and hear the forecast for Anchorage. The weatherman told him the prediction was for sixty-mile-an-hour winds on the Hillside. On the Hillside! The nearest edge of the Chugach Mountains to Anchorage, the Hillside was a residential community tucked into the near-wilderness. If it was going to blow like that in town, then it would blow with the power of a hurricane on McKinley.

Tejas scrambled to the doorway of his snow home and peeked outside. Whiteout. Tejas had to dig through his doorway, moving the flap of the parafoil out of the way. No moving that day. Or the next, either, it turned out. Two more days snowbound.

For hours Tejas sat sewing seams, patching his wind suit, doing minor repairs on his gear—he had cracked a goggle—and playing the harmonica. He played songs he usually played on the fiddle, played Scottish and Irish folk songs, played "Old Joe Clark." He played until his lips got sore and he couldn't raise his arms to jam anymore. That was a laugh—pinned down, forced to rest while the weather taunted him, he was more tired from harmonica playing than from climbing.

It was not always easy to adapt fiddle music to the harmonica, either. The more difficult the translation, actually, the better. That made him concentrate, and the concentration took his mind off his lack of movement. Besides, if it didn't sound good, who would care? There was no one around to criticize.

When he was younger, Tejas had hitchhiked all over the United States. Traveling light precluded carrying any large instrument, but a harmonica could fit into his pocket. He got lots of practice sitting by the side of the road waiting for rides. He found it a good way to amuse himself and later, when he was picked up, to amuse the drivers, too.

It certainly made more sense than carting his fiddle around in a big case. Fiddle playing had been part of him since he had bought one for $45 on a whim in a secondhand store somewhere in the Kentucky-Ohio area in the early seventies. He had no idea how to play it, but he taught himself slowly, made his own music. He missed the fiddle in the snow cave and wished he had it with him, but the harmonica would have to do.

When Tejas wasn't playing, he was eating. It is easy to lose weight at high altitude, especially under the strain of climbing. On rest days, Tejas still made sure he ingested 2,000 calories of oatmeal, nuts, cookies, beef jerky, dried fruit, chocolate bars, rice, potatoes, stuffing, noodles, meat, and vegetables. Usually, the hot food was all mixed together. "One-pot glop," Tejas called it. On climbing days, he ate 4,000 calories and he made sure to drink four quarts of fluids every day.

And when Tejas wasn't playing the harmonica or eating, he was thinking. Sooner or later the chores ended, the harmonica ran out of music, the appetite was satisfied, and there was nothing left but solitude. A man alone in the wild must like himself or he can become beset by demons. A man's temperament climbing solo is what drives him to continue, what gives him the courage to cow his own fears. An impatient man can't beat the mountain; it is always the mountain that dictates the terms, always the mountain that grants permission. A man must be patient. When the mountain says to wait, a man must wait.

As a child, Tejas's main sport was swimming. He dabbled in other sports, such as Little League baseball, and several members of his family enjoyed the outdoors through canoeing, kayaking and fishing. For years, though, Tejas swam for club teams his father, Phill Hansel, coached. He was still named Hansel in those days, too. He didn't change his last name until much later when, somewhat estranged from his father, he eventually took as his new name *Tejas,* an Indian word meaning "friendly" and the Spanish word for the state of Texas.

Young Vernon swam a lot; he raced, too, but never achieved much in the sport because he was competing with the other kids for his father's attention. He was a recalcitrant pupil, always challenging his father, hoping his dad would notice him in the gang of little swimmers. Rather than seeking to do his best to attract that notice, he frequently swam slowly on purpose. Provoking his father's ire was one way to get some attention, at least.

For years, Vern followed the black line on the bottom of the pool for hours a day. In those days there was nothing but Vern, the water, and the sounds of silence. Being underwater was so very like being underground, under the snow. Years of swimming trained Vern to cope with being alone with his own thoughts for hours.

"There's no input from outside," he said of being alone on a mountain. "There's just you. And it doesn't bother me. You just need the ability to be with yourself and not go bonkers."

Vern grew up in the Spring Branch section of Houston, surely one of the flattest places in the United States. There aren't any serious bumps on the land for hundreds of miles around. The skyline of downtown buildings was the closest thing to a mountain range in his early life.

Snow was something he saw only in books, or on television. When he was eight or nine, he remembers, it snowed about a half-inch, and he fantasized about building snow caves. The snow caves of his youth were actually not so different from the snow shelters he would use to survive on McKinley.

At thirteen, Vern became an Explorer Scout and spent a summer at the Philmont Boy Scout Ranch in New Mexico. It was there that he was first exposed to outdoor survival skills and first climbed mountains. The swimming had made his lungs strong, and he ran up and down those peaks, exhilarated by the outdoors and the heights.

Later, early in high school, Vern attempted his first solo of sorts: he ran away from home. He was determined to live in the woods and survive by trapping small animals for food. Someone told him the southwestern region of Colorado, near Durango, was the wildest, roughest area in the continental United States. That's all he needed to hear. Vern hitchhiked to Colorado and eventually reached this isolated region by bushwhacking over tough terrain and hiking up and over mountain passes at 11,000 feet for two and a half days. This will be terrific, he thought. No one would ever find him there. He could live off the land.

It seemed terrific all right. Until he got there. The wilderness area that others had called so rugged had gravel paths and bridges over streams. He was in a park! Reluctant to surrender his vision, he stayed anyway, camping in the woods for two weeks before giving up and heading back to Texas.

Vern had learned two things, two contradictory things, actually. He had learned that he could survive on his own. And he learned that he liked being with people.

He may have been comfortable with himself, may have been able to amuse himself, stay happy within himself more readily than the average person, but he also found he was very much a social animal. He never again sought the kind of solitude he had chased in Colorado, never attempted any elaborate solo missions again.

Until McKinley.

Motorcycle Hill

More dangerous steps.

In summer, the move from 11,000 feet to 14,000 feet, past the notorious Windy Corner—so named because of the ferocity of the breezes that snake around rock and blast climbers in the face—is a one-day climb.

The area between 11,000 and 12,000 feet on the West Buttress is called Motorcycle Hill. The terrain gets steeper and the snow is usually harder, more encrusted. Tejas had strapped crampons— the metal, sharp-toothed grips that climbers must have for traversing ice—on his boots. He weaved past crevasses, catching glimpses of dangerous holes that were often shrouded by blowing snow. He was wearing his ladder, but he was lucky. His eye was sharp, and though crevasses were often only ten feet from where he trod, his judgment was sound, so he did not have to test his homemade safety harness. It took intense concentration, though.

At the flat points on the glacier Tejas didn't expect to see big holes. Another comparatively safe point would usually be the bottom of the hill. In places where the elevation changed, though, he knew he was more likely to see spots where ice had been ripped apart. In those places there is a lot of stress, and the ground separates and shatters.

"That's a rule of thumb," said Tejas. "But crevasses can be anywhere. I ask myself, 'Are there any variations in the snow texture?' Then I get my ski pole out and start probing. I've been lucky, but I'm also very conservative."

There are always exceptions and always circumstances that surprise a climber no matter how careful he is. On the climb of Mount Logan in the Yukon Territory, Tejas was roped to two other climbers and walking between them. He fell into a crevasse and had to be hauled out. It was a sudden, chilling experience. One minute, Tejas was hiking along with his friends, the next he was hanging in a black hole, his gear weighting him down and threatening to strangle him. He first felt disoriented, then a touch afraid, but then, as he understood what had happened and that his partners would bring him up safely, he felt calm.

Tejas dangled in the crevasse for only fifteen minutes and had rescuers right there, but he said, looking back on it, that it seemed as if six days had passed before he was pulled out.

"It imprints itself quite deeply on the brain cells," he said.

Here, high on McKinley, Tejas's knowledge of the mountain helped. He knew the crevasses ran perpendicular to the pass above him. If he walked parallel to them, he would be okay, unless confronted by one he had to cross. He also planted wands in the snow to mark the locations of crevasses, in case he had to come by this area in a whiteout on the return trip.

Tejas skirted the biggest threat to his safety, the crevasses, with no mishap, but as he stepped forward gingerly, one slow step after one slow step on the incline, he faced a new problem. The crampons came loose. When he was halfway up the long hill, one slipped. He straightened it, but it kept giving, slipping partially off his foot. The crampons just wouldn't adhere to the fat, insulated overboots that protected his toes against the intense cold. He couldn't walk uphill on the hard snow without the crampons, though, so there was no question of what he had to do.

To solve the problem, he balanced on one foot and removed an overboot, then balanced on the other foot and removed the other one. All this while wearing his ladder.

Taking off the overboots created a new worry, though, and a new danger. Suddenly, his feet weren't warm enough. So periodically, Tejas stopped, leaned on his ski poles, and swung one foot hard, as if he were placekicking a football. One foot at a time, over and over, to get the blood flowing again.

The day was clear at first, and Tejas split up his equipment to make double hauls once again. With visibility, and with wands marking the crevasses, he decided that a second trip through the minefield of crevasses would not be difficult. But slowed by the continually annoying problem of the crampons, Tejas was caught in a position of having half his gear in one spot and half in another when the weather turned bad again. There was no choice. He had to make the second haul up the hill or risk losing important equipment.

The second trip was in blowing snow. Yes, it would have been one day to Windy Corner in summer, but not in weather like this. In weather like this, people stay home. They don't go for walks. At first Tejas couldn't even tell whether it was fresh snow falling, or whether the fifty-mile-an-hour wind was simply blowing old snow at him from Windy Corner. When he heard the kernels hit his parka, he knew they were ice particles picked up from the ground. Then, when they started landing softly, he knew they were fresh flakes. The legendary wind was picking up.

People talk of hundred-mile-an-hour winds at this spot on McKinley. Tejas said he was lucky. The winds he faced probably only had a strength of sixty miles an hour.

"You're walking right up into that," said Tejas. "From 12,500 feet, it just howls down. The wind blows so ferociously, the snow's blown away. I've seen rocks blowing across the glacier."

His goal was Windy Corner, but the change in weather and the damned crampons slowed his pace to a trudge.

As if he needed a reminder after fourteen climbs, Tejas was walking into the full might of the airstream that gives Windy Corner its name. This invisible enemy blasted, frozen and hard, right into his face as he worked his way up Motorcycle Hill.

Finally, as conditions worsened, he gave it up for the night, stopping not at 14,000 feet but at 12,500.

Camping safely and somewhat cozily above Windy Corner at 14,000 feet is natural. Camping at 12,500 is usually by accident and necessity. It seems to be an inviting place because it is flat, but it was not in Tejas's game plan for a reason. It is an exposed area and a frozen one. Tejas hates camping here. Only once before had he been forced to. "And we got our ass kicked then, too," he said.

There were remnants of old camps still on the large, open field where Tejas chose to make his latest snow shelter. He hoped that softer snow would have piled up on the lee sides of walls. He wanted to dig into snow, not ice, when he removed the shovel from his sled. He didn't want long delays; he wanted a place to get warm in a hurry. He dug the shovel into the snow. Six inches deep. Fine. A foot deep. Fine. Eighteen inches deep. Fine. But no deeper. The snow beneath was really more ice than snow, ice his shovel couldn't penetrate. So, laboring as his body grew chilled and the wind stole his breath, Tejas anxiously cut snow blocks. A construction worker on odd jobs many times in his life, Tejas knew how to build a wall. This time he built a wall a bricklayer would take pride in. The new house would not be as warm as his usual underground trenches, and it was certainly nothing that would ever be listed by Century 21, but it would keep him alive, he thought.

During the night the wind intensified. How hard, Tejas wondered, can the wind blow? It was not whistling, it was banging. Nonstop. He fell asleep, but the wind woke him. The parafoil was continually whipped, slapped hard and loud against the roof, almost the way a sail on a boat just catching a strong gust might ripple out.

Tejas lay in the shelter worried that the parafoil would rip off and blow away, leaving him more vulnerable to the wind.

At four A.M. Tejas put on his boots and went outside to see what the wind was doing to the shelter. In the pitch dark, and with crampons on his feet, and an ice ax to steady himself, he examined the V-shaped wall he had built in front of the snow house and was astonished to see how much it had eroded. The snow blocks were being sheared down. In eight hours one had been eaten almost all of the way through. The parafoil tarp had remained on the roof only because Tejas had placed 200 pounds of snow on top of it.

It was terribly risky to be outside at all in this kind of weather. Skin exposed just a few seconds could be frostbitten. And if he moved away from the sheltering wall of the snow house, the wind might lift Tejas right off of the mountain. Even with an ice ax and crampons, he was in danger.

"You can *probably* survive without your stuff on," he said. "But if you screw up, you could die, too. This is how mountaineers disappear."

Tejas had to rebuild the snow wall. If he didn't, the wind would just erode the snow the way ocean water lapping the shore devours a sand castle. Once that happened, he might freeze to death. He moved with great care, and to diminish the wind's impact on his body, Tejas crawled to where he had found the softer snow before he went to bed and cut new snow blocks.

An ice carver whose sculpture meant survival, he cut for hours. Once, a piece of ice, borne by the wind, struck him in the head. And above him, the sky was positively biblical. Instead of thunder and lighting, instead of the desert sands blowing, he had roaring, thunderous wind and arctic snow blowing. The clouds would rip apart and close, shift and close. The moonlight would thrust shafts of light on the snow, then disappear. It was crazy and distracting. Tejas feared being blown away, his body tossed into a snowy ravine where it would never be found. Yet, even so, he couldn't help admiring the sheer power and awesomeness of the scene.

He cut snow blocks, then molded them into a wall again and retreated once more from the great white. Outside, Tejas had worn layers that he had hoped would deflect the bite of the wind. He had on two pairs of polypropylene bottoms and a polypropylene top. He wore a pair of wind briefs over the bottoms for extra protection. He wore pile-weave bib overalls and a pile-weave jacket. Over that he wore a down parka and down pants. And finally, for the top layer, he wore a red windsuit with a fur-lined hood. But before pulling the hood over his head, Tejas also put on a ski mask, a polypropylene balaclava, ski goggles, and a hat with a chinstrap. He wore five layers on his feet, including thin dress socks, vapor-barrier booties, wool socks, a ten-pound pair of vapor-barrier boots called bunny boots, and nylon over-boots. He wore four layers of mittens on his hands.

That's the kind of packaging the well-dressed mountaineer needed on this mountain and Tejas knew it. He should have been protected against weather at least as cold as thirty degrees below zero, but he felt cold when he worked and stayed chilled when he climbed back into his shelter. The wind made twenty below feel like a hundred below.

"The first thing that comes to mind is treading water," said Tejas, likening battling cold to his swimming experiences. "You've got to keep working with it. You've got to maintain yourself at all times. If your feet get cold, you just can't let them go. If your hands get cold, you put them under your armpits.

"It's like gravity. It's continuous. It never stops. And it takes maintenance: just like when your car tires get worn down and you replace them. The actual process of freezing isn't too painful. It's in the moments before that when your body's actually scream-ing 'Take care of me!' "

Only the tip of his nose was exposed. It got frostbit. It stung like a sunburn.

Once back inside the shelter, Tejas warmed himself by keeping most of the clothing layers on and ducking into his three-tiered sleeping bag. When he heated water, he drank part of it to warm his innards and poured the rest into a container pressed against his feet to warm up his toes.

It worked. Gradually, he warmed up.

Tejas was safe again only because he had risked his life again. It would have been so easy to stay indoors, tucked into a com-paratively cozy and warm sleeping bag, assuming that the shelter would endure. He had wondered, "Why don't I just stay here?" But then he'd thought again. Tejas's innate prudence had over-come his laziness, had compelled him to dress and go outside.

"Because I made myself get out there," said Tejas, "I realized how close I was to death."

Vern vs. the Wind

Pinned down. Again. Still.

There was something funny about this whole thing. Here he was, isolated and alone on this wild mountain, and he couldn't even see it. Except for the area maybe six feet in front of his boots, Tejas hadn't actually seen the mountain he was climbing since he had landed on the Kahiltna Glacier. He knew the mountain so well, though, that never did he actually stray more than a hundred yards away from the path he was following.

Tejas matter-of-factly says that he knows McKinley intimately. He does not usually add that it is an intimacy born out of love. He will admit that, though.

"I've always been in love with it," said Tejas. "McKinley has always been the spirit of adventure and the symbol of Alaska for me. Just to look up at it in town gives me such a good feeling. When I'm flying around the state, I get my plane seats on the same side as McKinley. If I can, I even put off flying for a clear day."

So Tejas knows what McKinley looks like, even when he can't see it. On this day, when he ventured out of the snow shelter, Tejas could barely see anything.

He kept peeking out, kept creeping out. And for a whole day he kept retreating back inside. There was a great deal of time to think, particularly about this mountain that reminded him so often of its powers—this beautiful mountain that was trying to kill him, that hid itself under thicker and thicker layers of snow.

Mount McKinley is very much the coquette. The tourist who visits Alaska with visions of the famous Wonder Lake view dancing in his mind very often leaves disappointed. He may spend two, three weeks within range of McKinley, may actually go to Wonder Lake, some thirty miles from the mountain, but find the mountain staying in hibernation, hidden beneath thick cloud cover. In Anchorage, 130 air miles to the south, the residents speak of the mountain as they would the sun. "The mountain is out today," they say.

The mountain teased Tejas the very first time he ever saw it. And he came upon it by accident, the same way he came upon Alaska.

In the summer of 1973, hitchhiking around the United States and Canada, Tejas caught a ride from another young man pointing his van toward Alaska. Going to Alaska wasn't in Tejas's plans, but it wasn't out of them, either. He knew only that the last youth hostel listed in his guidebook was in Whitehorse, Yukon Territory.

"I figured I'd just head out," he said. "I had an inkling that maybe I'd end up in Alaska. I had an inkling I'd just go up to Dawson. I didn't really know my destination, but heading west from Whitehorse, there's only two places to go."

The driver was heading north to pick up a canoe he'd left in Circle, north of Fairbanks, along the Yukon; once that business was taken care of, they rode into Denali National Park. Deep inside the park, Tejas, the driver, and a third man stopped and went for a hike. This was perhaps thirty miles from McKinley itself, which at the time was totally blocked from view by clouds.

The Tejas reclining in his snow cave, bundled in layers of synthetic clothing, laughed at the memory of this. Fresh from the road, he had been a cowboy dressed for rodeo, not a climber for mountaineering. He'd been wearing jeans, a cowboy shirt, and a straw cowboy hat, his feet shod in leather cowboy boots. Tejas learned quickly what a fickle friend Alaska could be. It was early August. In early August in Texas the sun scorched and burnt. Here the sky darkened and snow fell thick and wet. A foot and a half of it.

All day Tejas and the two others slogged through this snow to the summit of a 5,000-foot peak. Tejas put on all the clothes he had, all of it cotton, and all of it soaked through. Wet and cold, Tejas began shivering uncontrollably. He became disoriented and began stumbling—early signs of hypothermia. They stopped to camp, and while Tejas paced, trying to stay warm, the others pitched a tent and built a fire. Hot tea and hot food finally stoked his own fire.

Tejas had been in the state only two days and it was trying to kill him.

The next morning, when they awoke from their exhaustion, the clouds lifted, gradually, slowly. The sun's rays poked through clouds and McKinley teasingly began to reveal itself in the distance.

From the stillness of night emerged the lush wildlife of McKinley habitat. Tejas saw fresh snow, fresh fox tracks. Nearby, two large caribou were grazing. They began running. Then they heard a sound and they stopped. A grizzly cub chewing on berries raised its head at the noise, and the bear began running—toward the men, whom it hadn't yet seen. The bear loped into a ravine and up the other side, facing them. One look at the human intruders and the bear did an abrupt about-face. He dashed back across the ravine, toward the caribou. The caribou turned and ran.

In the space of a few seconds, still rubbing sleep from his eyes, Tejas had seen more raw wildlife than he had ever seen before. He remembered thinking it was unbelievable, like being on television as part of *Wild Kingdom*. No one ever saw this kind of thing in person. And just as suddenly as this frenetic activity unfolded, the mountain came out in its full glory, offering tantalizing peeks. It took hours for the clouds to dissipate completely. It was almost as if a curtain were being raised. The mountain just grew, expanding and expanding. Part of the time Tejas just sat, staring, munching blueberries. Other times the men grew giddy together, flushed with the excitement of seeing this huge, imposing landscape emerge.

The men felt a sense of wonder. They had struggled to reach the summit of a puny little mountain only a day earlier; a baby mountain had almost defeated them.

As it teased him, Tejas thought of McKinley not merely as one giant skyscraper of a mountain. No. It was so big, so huge, that he thought of it as an entire skyline, an entire city, many cities strung together. This first sighting raised the emotion in his throat, blinded him with awe. But through the emotion, through the feeling and the blindness, he saw the future. Right then, right there, he told himself, and he told the others, "I'm gonna climb that."

There was no logic to that statement. Here he was, a newcomer in Alaska, not sure even that he would stay. Here he had been nearly beaten by a smaller hunk of rock. But something in him made Tejas blurt that out.

The climb didn't happen right away, though. Tejas was still a wanderer then. He hitchhiked in and out of the state over a period of a few years, stopping long enough to climb short mountains, to learn ice climbing, to understand winter camping in Alaska and winter mountaineering. And to make money working on the construction of the Trans-Alaska Pipeline at its terminus, in Valdez, 300 miles south of Anchorage.

The promise was never forgotten, but the opportunity never showed its face. The idea simmered quietly. Five years later the chance came. A roommate was scheduled to be an assistant guide on a McKinley climbing trip, and when another climber canceled, Tejas was invited in his place.

Tejas was anxious and excited. He was realizing his dream at last.

The first day on the Kahiltna Glacier he got violently ill; nausea, vomiting, diarrhea. At only 7,000 feet, he had altitude sickness. He wasn't even out of base camp and he was about to be placed on the next plane out, shipped home to recover. Tejas had the brief and depressing thought that this was one damn tough mountain. But his friend, Jim Hale, the trip leader, calmed him, made him drink water, and Tejas recovered quickly. He does admit that the incident probably contributed to his preferring to move up mountains slowly.

Now, when Tejas looks back at his sudden illness, he figures he simply overdid it the first day.

"It's my theory that altitude affects anyone who is straining too hard," he said. "I was trying to prove my worth because I was a last-minute addition."

It was a peculiar group Tejas that joined. There were seven others, and two of them, whom he hadn't known before, had coincidentally been swimmers for his father's club teams in Houston. One of those climbers was George Stransky, who had been the goalie on the United States Olympic water polo team in 1964 and is now in the U.S. Olympic Hall of Fame. On this climb, Tejas formed friendships that would last for years, and he began to understand the mountain and what it could throw at a man.

The West Buttress seemed like the toughest slope in the world to him then. Tejas felt like Sisyphus, the character in Greek mythology who would roll a rock up a hill only to see it roll right back down. Tejas put one foot in front of the other and, as he sank into the deep snow, felt as if he were slipping back twice as far. He climbed and said, "This will never end." He climbed and asked himself, "What am I doing here?"

The mountain roared and dumped snow on them, too, but somewhere on this hill the flatlander, who had almost been beaten by a 5,000-foot bump on the terrain five years before, found fresh lungs again and again, grew stronger and stronger. On summit day he wore his straw cowboy hat to the top and played "Oh, Susannah" on his harmonica.

He was on the roof of North America, 20,320 feet above sea level. He was a country boy in new country and proud of himself. Even if it was a grayout and the view was none too majestic, Tejas thought now, at last, he was a real Alaskan, no longer a Cheechako, but a Sourdough. "Hey," he thought, "this cowboy done good."

But not good enough, apparently.

Hale, a tall, broad-shouldered man who would later become a pastor in Talkeetna, but who perhaps at that point had more wildness in his soul, felt as fresh as the day they'd begun. Hale had a gleam-in-his-eye proposal. He'd never been on the north summit. How about it? Tejas had grown fresher, not weaker. Indeed, how about it?

Leaving the others behind, Tejas and Hale set off to attempt a rare doubleheader. They dropped down to a rock band at 18,200 feet where Denali Pass is, and felt their way around the rocks, sneaking in and out, around curves, scrambling. They didn't really know where they were going; they just tested a route as they went.

"We weren't sure about distance or anything," said Tejas. "So we walked across the plateau, and there was a serac, some rocks, and then we said, 'Well, let's go up this and see if we can see where the summit would be.' "

Boom, they were at the summit ridge. Fifteen more minutes to the high point, they figured. Didn't even know where it was. Well, this is the high point, they guessed. They must be there. This cornice is probably it. Wonder what it looks like down the other side?

The other side was the Wickersham Wall, at over 13,000 feet the greatest sheer vertical gain on a mountain in the world. Not even Mount Everest has a wall that extends that high from base to summit.

Tejas and Hale wondered what it looked like and wanted to know. So Tejas held Hale by the feet and let him look over the edge. And then Hale held Tejas by the feet and let him look over the edge. They looked straight down.

"It was pretty impressive," said Tejas.

Children, don't do this at home.

Hale had a dry description for what they did that day. He called it "an unorthodox procedure."

On that day in 1978, they did the north and south summits in about eight hours. Tejas left the mountain beaming.

"Doing both in the same day, I felt like I was coming into my own," he said.

But he didn't feel so exuberant lying in his snow shelter on McKinley this day ten years later. He wasn't coming into his own, wasn't going anywhere at all. His only travels were in his thoughts.

The wind howled outside. How long would it last?

And where was Lyon?

On the Move

A skilled mountaineer learns to read the wind, the sky, and the climate almost as well as a meteorologist. He must because his life may depend on it. Moving at the wrong time may put him in danger. Moving at the wrong time may mean that his goal, the summit, will never be reached.

Tejas was antsy. He had been on the mountain for about two weeks already and he was only a few thousand feet above base camp. His original plan had called for him to be on or nearing the summit by now. But he was no fool, either. He was willing to take risks if they were worthy risks, but he wasn't willing to take stupid risks. To have ventured out on the previous days would have involved taking stupid risks.

So he had lain in his snow shelter, nibbling on his food supplies at half the normal rate, wishing the weather away. On days when he climbed, Tejas consumed about 4,000 calories. He needed that kind of fuel because the work of plodding up the side of this very tough mountain burned them up rapidly. He gorged himself on the kind of goodies a man going about his routine business at sea level would have to pass up—or become a blimp. Gail had baked a large batch of oatmeal cookies with cinnamon, cloves, and chocolate chips. Tejas had no trouble coaxing himself to eat many of those. He preferred to eat tasty things, things he would have eaten if he were at home, and he tried to limit his intake of the prepackaged meals that are so easy to carry but so tiresome to the palate.

"I like to go with quality foods," said Tejas. "I'm the one who's doing the eating, so it's nice to have some good quality. I'm always conscious of my weight on a climb like that, not wanting to lose too much."

For his main courses, Tejas went heavy on the starches. His dinners featured noodles, spaghetti, macaroni, and potatoes. He tried to rotate them so that he wouldn't get too bored with the menu. He always mixed in vegetables and some meats for flavoring and extra sustenance. He ate hearty breakfasts of French toast, pancakes, powdered eggs, and hot and cold cereal.

Tejas figured he should eat 4,000 calories per day on a day when he was moving and fighting the hill and the elements. But he also knew that it would be easy to eat that much or more when sitting still, at least partially out of boredom, and thereby zip through supplies that might be needed later.

Climbers who stay very long at high altitude, particularly above 25,000 feet in the Himalayas, burn calories at a much higher rate. It takes a lot of energy just to breathe when they are that high. At that altitude breathing is actually so much work that a man asleep is still working his lungs harder than at sea level.

On one previous trip to McKinley in 1983, when Tejas essentially climbed the mountain twice in one visit, he lost ten pounds. In 1982, on a long ski traverse in the Wrangell–St. Elias Range of Alaska, Tejas also lost ten pounds. In Argentina, when he climbed Aconcagua three times in just over a week, he lost fifteen pounds. If he lost fifteen pounds on this climb of McKinley, he feared, he would lose too much strength. Being trapped because of the weather was a plus: it gave Tejas additional rest, it didn't sap his strength, and it limited the weight loss to a few pounds in the early going. On days when he rested, when he couldn't move out of his snow shelter at all, Tejas tried to eat no more than 2,000 calories a day.

The climb of McKinley on the West Buttress involved hiking sixteen miles from base camp to the summit. Tejas had climbed for ten miles on snow and ice. He had gone far, but he hadn't gotten very high. It was still some 7,500 feet to the top.

Experience on McKinley meant reading McKinley's winds, knowing how much wind was too much. And how much is that?

"Generally, when you can hear it underground in your sleeping bag," said Tejas.

That's wind.

"If I could hear it outside, I'd blow that day off," he said. "Forty miles an hour for winter mountaineering is pretty bitter. Thirty miles an hour is pretty tough.

"I've had McKinley climbs where we had the whole group fighting the wind. The food and fuel were up there and we had to get there. There's real potential for hypothermia or frostbite. You can't stop to eat or to drink. You've just got to slug it out."

On the third day in this camp, the sound of the wind changed. By everyday city standards it was still a big-time blow. By Mount McKinley standards it was a strong breeze. It was probably minus-twenty degrees with the wind blowing twenty-five to thirty miles per hour, Tejas figured. But that was an improvement, and he couldn't stay in this camp forever. To stay too long meant quitting the climb. To stay in one spot waiting for a perfect day might mean waiting until spring. This was not, after all, a weekend outing at the shore. He expected Mount McKinley in winter to be temperamental.

"You say, 'Shucks, time to move on,'" Tejas said of his mood.

Yes, time to move on. If he could work outside cutting snow blocks, he could move outside hauling a sled; as long as the wind had calmed sufficiently to assure him that he wouldn't be blown off the mountain. Plus, Tejas knew this from all of his experiences of McKinley: the wind could blow for days and days at this spot. He knew 12,500 feet was a bad place. If he waited for the wind to truly subside, he really might wait forever. But if he climbed, he might climb above the wind, above Windy Corner, and snuggle beneath a protected wall. Tejas was somewhat rested, and sitting there twiddling his thumbs for a few hours didn't sound appealing, never mind for still another day. He made the decision to head up.

Windy Corner, at 13,200 feet, is a long ramp that gets progressively steeper. It's an edge of rock sticking out from the West Buttress, and the wind rips off it.

"It screams in your face right down from the corner," said Tejas.

What he was counting on to get himself higher on the hill was his experience on the mountain coupled with his ability to understand the weather patterns that swirled around it. He knew that if he could climb above Windy Corner, there was an excellent chance the wind would die down. How could he have known this? By studying weather maps? He knew it because he had lived it before.

"Every time I've gone around Windy Corner in the wind," he said, "it's only at the corner where it's really windy. A little bit beyond that, it's relatively calm.

"I knew I could get out of this if the wind cooperated. I'm not sure how many days after I got out of it (at 12,500 feet) it was still blowing there."

Tejas packed his sled with half his gear and trudged out of camp—wary, but moving steadily. One foot in front of the other would get him there, he knew. He felt good about moving again, even if it was slow movement. The wind whipped at him, but he knew he had made the right choice. Yes, it was cold. Yes, it took effort, but it was far more rewarding than lying still, trapped in one place.

Little did Tejas realize how beneficial movement could be. Just a short distance beyond his camp he spied an old wand stuck in the snow. Pulling out his shovel, he dug around beneath the wand and found what for him was buried treasure. Not the jewels and silver pirates sought when they followed ancient maps, but something even more valuable: a food cache left behind by a summer expedition. There was four days' worth of food stored under the snow and a gallon of gas that he could use for fueling his stove. This made up for some of the depletion of his own supplies, forced on him by the weather.

Buoyed by his discovery, Tejas worked his way up the mountain—directly into a new danger zone. At about 13,000 feet the crevasses are plentiful and frequently masked by blowing snow. It is an area Tejas knew well. In clear weather a crevasse was a big enough threat, but windy conditions could spread a blanket of freshly blown snow over the deepest holes. Tejas moved with extreme caution. Only the summer before, a friend and fellow Genet Expeditions guide, Norma Jean Neumeister, had fallen into a crevasse in this area. Neumeister was safely roped to another climber at the time and was pulled out of the crevasse without serious injury, but her description of the hole as a seemingly bottomless void was very vivid in Tejas's mind as he edged his way through this minefield of danger. He recognized the crevasse where Neumeister had fallen in and he recognized the distinctive depressions that new snow covering a crevasse can make as he came upon others.

The previous summer, Tejas had led three guided climbs of McKinley. By that time, he was at least toying with the idea of a solo winter climb, so he climbed with the future in mind.

"I was eyeballing things, asking, 'Where is this located? How far is it from here to there? How wide is this crevasse?' Scoping things out, saying, 'Is this doable?' Of course, I was looking at it from a perspective that nobody else would. But being conservative, more conservative than many people, I had to feel very comfortable with what I was getting into before I could actually go for it.

"Whereas somebody with a more brash life-style, somebody a little bolder than I was, might have felt very comfortable doing it without having as much knowledge of the mountain as I had, I was working with a tremendous advantage over anybody else who was even going to attempt it. Of the people who had attempted such a climb, I had the most knowledge."

Now he had to use that knowledge. Once again, the aluminum ladder was Tejas's only companion. It was the only security he had, but that was in case of emergency. It was nice to have it, he thought, but it would be nicer to avoid emergencies altogether.

Every mountain climber knows the objective dangers he faces on his trip, and he prepares for them. And every mountain climber knows the famous horror stories of those who disregarded the danger of crevasses or were beaten by them despite the most careful precautions. The *Minus 148* expedition was almost halted at its start because of a crevasse fatality. Famed American mountaineer Jim Wickwire, of Seattle, lost a climbing partner during a training climb on McKinley. Almost every season on McKinley one or more recreational climbers—usually Europeans, who are more used to climbing in the Alps than on deadly peaks like McKinley—are killed in crevasse accidents.

"Even on a rope I'm probably one of the more conscientious people going through a crevasse field, because crevasses scare the beans out of me," said Tejas.

Above 13,000 feet Tejas was confronted by a strange and different climate: it was clear. His guess that things would improve if he got out of the wind zone had been accurate. He hauled his first sled load up to 13,500 feet and dumped it there. The only problem he had now was that he had to go back down for the other half of his gear and cart it back up through the same minefield. Yet repeating the route was not nearly so difficult as making it the first time. The steps were fresh in his mind, he had placed wands to help guide himself, and he knew where those crevasses were now. Tejas negotiated his way through the snow a second time and made camp at 13,500 feet.

"Again, knowledge of the mountain pays off," he thought.

If he had waited at 12,500 until it cleared, he might not have advanced at all that day.

"I was in the right spot when it got clear," he said.

Tejas was very pleased with himself when he went to sleep that night. He was making progress again.

More Snow

Tejas began the day with big plans.

He hoped to climb past 14,000 feet and begin the climb up the head wall of McKinley's West Buttress. This is commonly called the crux of the climb on the West Buttress route. It is the place on this route that is the steepest, and where the climbing is truly climbing, not hard hiking, though Tejas insists it isn't all that hard.

"It looks like a ninety-degree wall, but it's not," he said. "It psychs people out. You say, 'Oh, here's where the climbing begins,' but it's not all that hard. It's slow."

One reason it's slow is that it's dangerous. The climber needs ropes, crampons, ice ax, everything he has that enables him to dig into ice and snow, including his full powers of concentration, because a slip here means a fall down a sheer wall with no soft piles of snow to cushion bounces, or to slow a tumbling body.

But Tejas didn't get too far. The weather had the final say again. By the time he got to 14,000 feet, he was once more completely socked in. He might as well have been a ship dry-docked by fog.

That meant only one thing: building another snow shelter and going underground to wait again. The wind rose and the temperature dropped, once again falling well below zero. McKinley was proving to be more demanding, more challenging with its violent winter moods, than Tejas had expected. This whole expedition was supposed to take only sixteen days round-trip. It was sixteen days already and he'd barely gotten anywhere. Or at least it seemed that way.

At this point in the climb, though, Tejas had something else to do to occupy himself besides playing his harmonica. It was time to make a few decisions. Tejas needed to spend some time sorting through his equipment, deciding which items were still of use for the climb to the summit and which things would be of value only on the way down from here.

Much of the gear that Tejas had packed and hauled was for use between the Kahiltna Glacier and this spot. At 14,000 feet, at the head wall, the terrain changes. The danger of slipping into a crevasse diminishes the higher on the mountain one climbs. Those big, gaping holes that are so frightening near Windy Corner pretty much disappear at higher altitude.

Tejas no longer needed his ladder. From here on it would be more of a burden than a help, so he found a parking place for it. He stood it straight up against a wall, so that it wouldn't get buried under fresh snow.

The sled, too, would be more burden than benefit higher up. It was a great tool for pulling 150 pounds of equipment across the snow, but it wasn't very practical to strap it on his back and take it with him.

The choice of what would stay and what would come with him was fairly straightforward. There was a temptation to take everything he had to eat. Tejas figured he had six or seven days' worth of food, and the way things were going he might need it before he even glimpsed the summit. But he also wanted to have something to come back to in a real emergency, so he cached some food and fuel just in case.

Joining the ladder and sled were his ski poles. They, too, were terrific for plodding across drifted snow, but they weren't quite so handy on steeper ground where he could kick steps into packed snow. Climbing utensils—wands, ice ax, pickets (metal stakes), and hand-held ascenders that would clip onto rope and grip it to help him lift his body up the wall—were all coming along with him. Anything big and bulky that wouldn't fit in his pack was not.

Tejas indulged himself by toting his citizens band radio, his transistor radio, and his harmonica with him. None were necessary for survival, but all were important for peace of mind. His one compromise was to leave some of his extra batteries in the cache.

When he finished his unpacking and repacking, Tejas had a pack that weighed about fifty pounds. Fifty pounds was manageable. He could carry that. He had carried heavier, but he knew his limits.

Jim Hale, Tejas's old climbing buddy, remembers one backcountry trip they took together when Tejas was carrying ninety pounds' worth of equipment in his backpack. Carrying the weight wasn't a problem because Tejas had such strength in his forearms and shoulders. But Hale recalled Tejas experimenting with a different way to lift the pack off the ground to put it on his back. Slipping the straps over his arms and slowly squirming into the pack seemed too complicated.

"Vern flipped the pack over his head and it landed with a thunk on his shoulders," said Hale. The pack dropped on Tejas's shoulders with its full weight all at once. "It almost drove him into the ground. There was a look not of shock but of amazement on his face. Had it been anybody less, it would have broken his shoulders off."

Tejas, as he does in approaching any task, went about separating his equipment very methodically. Whenever Tejas goes on a major climb, he plans meticulously, studies all available information, and reviews all potential situations in his mind repeatedly. For an adventurer, for a man who undertakes tremendous physical challenges, Tejas does not behave in an impulsive manner.

Harry Johnson, Tejas's boss and the owner of Genet Expeditions, said Tejas has the goals of a Type A personality but is actually a Type B.

"Vernon happens to like to climb very slowly," said Johnson, who himself has scaled McKinley five times, though never in the winter. "That's his meticulous, careful style."

Tejas will concede that maybe he is a Type B personality, if there is such a thing.

"I'm not really driven," he said, "but I'm not limited. I don't limit myself. I'm not consumed by desire, but I have a consuming desire to push, to find my own limits, whether or not it's on McKinley. There's a drive to live life fully."

Johnson, a close friend of Tejas's who has also climbed the highest peaks on other continents, such as Aconcagua, Kilimanjaro in Africa, and Elbrus in the Soviet Union, and also has parasailed off the summits of mountains, called Tejas a "pretty safe guy."

"I consider Vernon just as crazy as I am," said Johnson, "but I've never done anything with him that wasn't within the margin of safety. He takes very calculated chances."

The average person on the street will always have difficulty understanding that distinction. After all, to the average person, the mere idea of climbing McKinley in winter is not within the margin of safety. It is beyond contemplation.

Working slowly, it took Tejas only a few hours to sort out what he needed to advance. He was ready to go. However, the weather wasn't ready to let him.

It would have been easy to say he was going up, and to hell with the weather. But one thing Tejas had was patience. He was frustrated once again, but he was not so frustrated that he would go on at any cost. He had only himself to answer to. Wherever Lyon was, and whatever he was doing, Tejas couldn't allow him to influence his decision. It would have been a departure from his entire climbing background for Tejas to move against the wind just for the sake of moving. He attempted to abide by roughly the same standard of gauging weather for himself that he would have used guiding clients on the mountain. He tried to apply the same criteria to the decision of whether or not to move.

Tejas always thinks back to his first-ever climb of McKinley. He remembers that he had actually enjoyed making it. Hale, the chief guide, had made the trip pleasurable by telling jokes and setting an appropriate, easy-going pace.

Tejas remembers that he enjoyed being in Hale's company. He

thinks Hale was a guide model worth emulating, and he always tries to remember that the climb should be fun as well as hard work.

To Tejas, that means communicating to a client that it's important to get satisfaction from the experience of being on the mountain, even if the summit is never reached.

"The summit is not the ultimate goal," says Tejas. "The ultimate goal is to enjoy and come down with all your fingers and toes. And Jim Hale told me on that first trip there's no mountain anywhere on earth that's worth a little toe or one finger."

Those were words Tejas tried to live by in his job, when he had the responsibility of caring for and making judgments for other, less experienced climbers, and he tried to live by those tenets now under trying circumstances.

He had always believed that it was more important to keep his health than to capture the prize. If others in the climbing community were more gung ho, more willing to take the chances at the risk to their health, that was fine for them, but Tejas looked at it from a less macho perspective.

"It's a better challenge, a finer challenge, to climb to the top and come back with everything than to gut it out and be a he-man, fight nature, and in the process lose something," said Tejas. "So what? You've got bragging rights, but you don't have any fingers."

Perhaps it might seem to make sense for a moment, to be worth it in trade for the top, but he knew that afterwards it would make no sense at all.

Other men have looked at it differently. For them, the fame that accompanies a triumph of a first on one of the world's most respected and impressive peaks is worth the pain and suffering that might come with it, too. Men have forfeited fingers and toes to climb the world's deadliest mountains and considered it worthwhile. Tejas couldn't see it.

"The accomplishments in mountaineering are so intangible anyway that to do it and lose something . . ." Tejas's voice trailed off as he considered his fingers. "To commit yourself to the point that you're going to lose something," he resumed, "or come back scarred from the experience, or even die—that goes beyond a good reason for being there. My primary goal is to live my life fully and enjoy it, not end up losing it."

Bob Seibert, a National Park Service ranger, said that being alone on McKinley in winter, when there are no other people within miles, must be a fearsome experience. Only someone very much at peace with himself could handle it.

Clearly, Tejas had made his peace before attempting the climb. He knew what was wise and what was not, knew what he was willing to attempt and what he was not. He believed in himself, believed he had sufficient winter mountain experience, altitude experience, and route experience.

"I felt I had a real chance to do it and come back with my fingers and toes," he said.

Tejas tried to draw something positive from his delays, draw something good out of being trapped in one place by vicious, screaming wind and blowing snow. On his summer climbs he had often spent an extra day resting at 14,000 feet, though that was primarily because he usually took his guided groups from 11,000 feet to that height in a single day—a big jump for people who are often giving their bodies the biggest challenge of their lives. At least this time Tejas could comfort himself with the knowledge that it was a familiar camp, and one he might have stopped at anyway.

Tejas never truly lost patience on his way up the mountain. He was not happy that he kept running into storms, but the excitement of the adventure itself kept his adrenaline pumping, even when the weather threw his schedule off.

"It was still fun," he said. "You can't control the weather, but you can wait for it."

Tejas also knew that his next move, because of the ruggedness of the headwall, would bring him at least to 16,000 feet, a mark of progress that would take him 2,000 climbing feet closer to the summit.

Of course, that was if he ever got to move. His guided climbs ordinarily take a week to reach the 14,000-foot level. Tejas had faced so much rotten weather on his solo that it had taken him over two weeks.

As he settled down in his brand-new snow shelter for some

more rest that he didn't want, or feel he needed, Tejas had an idle thought. He had told pilot Lowell Thomas to come get him in sixteen days. Sixteen days was tomorrow, March 2. He sure wasn't going to be finished climbing in one day. And he sure wasn't going back to base camp to say hello to Lowell, either.

Specters

As usual, Tejas was ready before the weather was ready. Would the weather ever be ready when he was? He wasn't going anywhere with the wind blasting at what—forty, fifty, sixty, or more miles an hour?

The wind roared all day long on March 2 and all day long on March 3. These were the moments of the climb that tested him mentally, just as hauling loads of 150 pounds tested him physically. It wasn't easy just sitting there using up food and fuel. He was rested and anxious, but he remembered well, and was reminded daily, that the mountain was the boss, the mountain was in charge.

"If it's not in the cards," said Tejas, "it's not in the cards."

A philosophical attitude was a must. If he didn't roll with the punches, he might make a mistake. Sure, he thought, it was a setback when the wind blew for long stretches, but he willed himself to be strong. "I can deal with that," was his constant reminder to himself. "I'll do what it takes. I'll see if I can go a little farther."

On some of the days, Tejas could go no farther. If he had tried to climb the headwall, he would have been blown away, would have been lifted off the ice and had his body dumped into a crevasse or gully somewhere else on the mountain. He would have been dead and his body never found. Like Naomi.

It was hard not to think about Uemura. From here up, thoughts of Uemura drifted in and out of Tejas's mind with startling regularity. Sometimes he thought of him consciously, and other times he sensed his presence. A little higher on the mountain, above 17,000 feet, Tejas camped where Uemura had camped, and once, in the middle of the night, Tejas awoke feeling a breeze.

"I said, 'Good morning, Naomi,' in Japanese," recalled Tejas. "I sensed his presence in the cave. Part of this might have been an altitude hallucination, but it still remains real to me."

When rescuers searched for Uemura, they first found evidence at 14,000 feet. He, like Tejas, had left some gear before climbing the headwall. He never made it this far down again to pick it up.

It was hard for Tejas not to think of himself being with Uemura as he traced his route. They were kindred spirits. They were both mountaineers willing to risk their lives, willing to challenge the worst Mount McKinley could offer. Uemura, so much more renowned than he, so tough, so experienced, had been in this situation. He had been buffeted by violent winds and pinned down by angry storms, had lived many of the last days of his life underground, under snow, waiting out the brutal weather.

Only somewhere, Naomi had not waited. Somewhere he had been caught by the wicked weather. Somewhere, somehow, the wind, the weather, and the mountain had conspired together and beaten him, taken his life, his body. But not his spirit. The spirit of Uemura was strong in Tejas. Many times when he lay awake in his snow shelter, he thought of the Japanese adventurer, thought of the trail Uemura had carved for him.

In the void where no human voices penetrated, in the silence of loneliness, when his thoughts drifted away from the loving arms of his girlfriend Gail, when they drifted away from the comradeship he had shared with other climbers, Tejas's thoughts settled on Uemura.

84

He turned it over and over in his mind. Where had Uemura died? How had Uemura died? He had stumbled upon no clues to tell him. Of course, what was to be seen on a mountain coated so thickly with heavy layers of snow? What was to be seen in a place where the wind lifted the top layer of covering of snow every few minutes and replaced it with a new layer of snow? Who could tell anything here?

Tejas recalled the drama and the emotion of his visit to Japan in 1984.

"I'd thought more about Japan in the previous two weeks than I had in two years," he said.

And each step of the way on the trip, in the plane, on the glacier, on the mountain, fresh thoughts of Uemura, what he had done, and what he had not done, broke in on Tejas's thoughts. The higher Tejas inched on the mountain, the more he thought about Uemura.

"I felt his spirit up there," said Tejas. "That's where his spirit dwells. I had the feeling he was sharing the mountain with me. His spirit was one of a loner who was searching for the ultimate challenge."

The spirit gave Tejas encouragement, but it never encouraged him beyond what his judgment told him was the right move to make. Perhaps Uemura had been a trifle bolder, a trifle more reckless. Perhaps Tejas took a bit more care in one certain way than Uemura did. As Tejas cursed the foul weather that once again had locked him in place and tried his patience, he could speculate that perhaps his patience was the one certain assurance that he took more care than Uemura.

But every time his prospects for advancing on the mountain dimmed, Tejas had a lucky breakthrough. Of course, he was making his own luck. A climber has to climb above the wind or a storm to be in position for luck. It wouldn't do any good to have a break in the weather if you were mired at base camp, but if you had pushed a bit and put yourself high, clearing weather might give you the shot at the summit you were after.

"That's what I call luck, but it's planned," said Tejas. "It's doing everything you can do to get luck on your side."

So over and over as he waited in his snow shelter, with time dragging on and his food supply dwindling, Tejas repeated to himself that he knew this mountain and understood its ways, and he would use that knowledge to make the right moves.

He knew that the weather would not stay terrible for a month. That just didn't happen. The weather never stays terrible for a month. It couldn't snow forever, right? He had never seen it this bad, but always he expected the weather would break.

"And fortunately, I was able to wait it out," he said.

Yes, Tejas had patience. Perhaps it would be the one thing that would bring him back home alive.

Radio Contact

Sometime in the night, the wind subsided. Its howl, its roar, was absent. No longer were its waves crashing in Tejas's head. He woke up to the sound of a quiet mountain. Lying there, under the snow, he was peaceful. Today, Tejas felt sure, he would move. The mountain and the weather would let him climb.

Then, as he prepared his pack, as he prepared to move, he heard something. It was faint at first, then slightly louder, and Tejas recognized the sound. It was the buzzing noise the hard-working engines of a small plane make. He knew that sound very well. The plane sounded distant, much lower on the mountain than he was. He thought it was perhaps just above the Kahiltna Glacier, flying over the pass there.

The sound faded out, like a lost radio signal. But then there it was again, just as before, buzzing in the distance at first, then ever closer. Slowly, Tejas realized the plane was circling the mountain. And if it was circling the mountain, it was probably looking for him. It might be Lowell. He scrambled to grab his citizens band radio and inserted the batteries.

Tejas talked into the radio: "Anybody got a copy out there?"

Anybody did. Roger Robinson's voice broke through the clouds onto Tejas's radio.

"Yeah, Vern, go ahead," he said.

Robinson was in a small plane with bush pilot Eric Denkewalter, and they wanted to know how he was doing.

The park rangers had been anxious. They had heard nothing from Tejas for so long. They had been rooting for him on this historic climb; they knew him, cared about him, wanted him back home safely. As each day passed with no word, as the mountain stood shrouded in thick clouds and snow, they were as trapped on the outside looking in as Tejas was trapped in his shelters. Small planes couldn't penetrate this kind of weather, so they couldn't look for him and couldn't tell where he was on the mountain. They could only guess that he would be well above base camp.

This day, though, the clouds had disappeared and a decision was made to see where Tejas was.

"For once, the weather was good," said Robinson. "I knew where Vern would probably be, so we started high. We couldn't see base camp, and we spent a lot of time trying to find Vern's cache. We went up to 17,000 feet. We figured if we circled long enough, we'd raise him out of his snow cave. When you're in a snow cave, you don't hear a lot of things.

"We stayed there and circled, maybe ten times. We couldn't see any trace of Vern, and then he finally came on the radio. It was good to hear his voice."

Tejas was thrilled to hear them.

"I'm at fourteen," Tejas told them. "I'm doing okay. I've got enough food and I'm going up."

"Good," replied Robinson. "You sound great."

"What about Lyon?" Tejas asked. He wanted to know about Lyon. His heart was pounding. Had Lyon made the summit? Was this what Roger would tell him? "Where is Geoffrey?"

Robinson could detect the anxiety in Tejas's tone. He was matter-of-fact in his answer.

"Oh, Lyon is out of here."

Only then did Tejas discover that Lyon was long gone, had been off the mountain for days. His climb was really only between himself and McKinley, with no competitors racing up its frozen flanks. It really was a solo.

Later, Tejas would recall how he felt. "I realized, 'Good, I don't even have to think about him anymore.' "

Tejas was just as concerned about the food cache he'd left buried at base camp. That was the food he was counting on if he had to wait to be picked up. After all the snow of the last couple of weeks, he feared it would be buried so deeply that he'd ski right past and never find it. He asked Robinson and Denkewalter to search for his stuff.

Now that the weather had broken, Tejas said, he was going to move out of camp and try to climb to 17,200 feet, where one of the regular high camps on the mountain was, before nightfall. He told Robinson he had enough food for five more days with him. And then the conversation, which probably lasted only three minutes, ended.

"It was fairly brief," said Robinson. "I figured on making it as short as possible to save his batteries."

As soon as he signed off, though, Tejas was kicking himself.

"Why didn't we talk for a while?" That was Tejas's feeling. "It was too official. I wanted to say, 'Hey, Roger, fly around a little. Let's shoot the bull. What's going on in town?' " Tejas had even forgotten to ask Robinson to say hello to Gail Irvine and tell her he was all right. He hoped Robinson would go right back to Talkeetna and phone her.

"It was important to me that people knew I was okay," Tejas said later.

Robinson took care of that. He did call Gail.

"I kept in fairly frequent contact," said Irvine. She was thrilled when Robinson telephoned. Everything had been a blank until then—no contact, no word. "There was tremendous relief. Being out of touch is hard. And it was past the time he was expecting to come out."

Tejas said, "I should have talked a lot longer. I had the batteries for it." But he felt good: he had talked with a friend for the first time in almost three weeks, he knew that Lyon wouldn't beat him to the summit, and the weather was cooperating.

When he turned off the radio, Tejas looked up. The sun was glimmering through the clouds.

Triple Jeopardy

In good weather during the prime McKinley climbing season, the climb from 14,000 feet, at the base of the headwall, to 16,000 is a full, strenuous day. It encompasses what can be nerve-wracking steps up the headwall for an inexperienced climber, even though he's being coaxed along and relying on a guide for help. Climbers arrive in camp exhausted, but proud of themselves.

Climbing by himself, with his first help from the weather in many a day, Tejas felt certain he would be able to climb even higher and possibly reach the 17,200-foot camp.

He was wrong. It took Tejas two thirds of the day to move up from 14,000 to 15,400 feet.

As Tejas climbed, he stepped very carefully, and his caution proved necessary. He encountered four major crevasses. Tejas was not especially surprised to see these gaping holes, but he had left his ladder at 14,000 feet, so he was without his major source of protection against crevasse danger. Without being tied to another climber and without the ladder, any slip could be fatal.

Tejas was not foolish enough to cross the crevasses unroped and unprotected. The only alternative left for him was to employ what Tejas calls the triple-rope technique.

Before reaching the first crevasse, Tejas removed a three-foot, one-pound metal picket from his pack and drove the stake into the ground. The lightweight pickets are designed to hold a man's weight, but once again using extreme caution, Tejas moved ahead five more feet and planted a second picket in the ground.

Tejas then tied himself onto a rope with an ascender, a piece of mountaineering gear that gives a climber both maximum freedom of movement and maximum protection. The hand-held ascender could be used to grip the rope or be squeezed open to permit the climber to slide along the rope. If the climber loses his grip, the ascender grabs the rope for him and halts his movement.

Tejas had never actually practiced the triple-rope maneuver before coming to McKinley, but he had studied the concept and felt sure a situation would come up where he would have to use it.

"Hanging from two of those, you're not going to go very far if a snow bridge collapses," he said of the pickets.

In this way, Tejas advanced. If he fell into a crevasse, if a snow bridge he walked across decided to collapse, the ascender would dig into the rope and stop his rapid slide, and then the pickets driven into the snow would hold his weight. He would still be in a hole, literally, but his fall would be arrested and he would still be alive. It would be up to him to pull himself out of the hole.

"It isn't a good situation," said Tejas, "but it's a lot better than going to the bottom."

Tejas crossed the first crevasse safely, then drove a fresh picket into the ground and spaced another new one five feet beyond. Once anchored safely there, Tejas reversed his ground and went back over the snow bridge to where he had placed the first pickets. He yanked them out of the snow and crossed the snow bridge and crevasse still a third time, feeling that this time, at least, there was little danger of a fall.

It was tedious work, but there was no other way—no other way to ensure that each fresh step he took was as safe as the last step he had taken. And he had some luck, too. For once, the weather was more a friend than a foe. No snow, only few clouds, and some sun. It was semiclear all the time, at least. Plus, on this part of the mountain, the wall itself guards against the wind. So at this point, where Tejas had to concentrate, had to use both wits and strength to traverse the danger zone, he didn't have to worry about bad weather.

"It was cooperative," he said. "Another place I needed good weather."

Tejas repeated the procedure three more times. Besides the walking time, Tejas estimated it took a half hour or more to cross each crevasse, quite a slow pace to cover perhaps ten yards each time. But this was no time, no place, to lose patience.

"I was doing all this with mittens," said Tejas. "I had to be seriously patient."

And this figured to be the easiest part. He wasn't even truly on the headwall yet.

In the spring and summer, when McKinley is as populated as a small village, when guided group after guided group attempts the summit, climbers are aided by fixed ropes on the headwall. Rather than lay fresh rope for each climb, the guiding groups are permitted to leave in place ropes that are known to be reliable. It takes work to implant the ropes, and it can be dangerous work. If each group were required to lay new ropes, the climbers' progress would be slowed, and there might be more injuries to inexperienced mountaineers.

Tejas was counting on using the fixed ropes to make it up the headwall safely. There was just one thing: once he passed over the crevasses and reached the spot at about 15,000 feet where 1,000 feet of fixed ropes should have been, he couldn't find them.

"The lower two-hundred-fifty feet were buried," he said. "I never did find them."

So accustomed to the way the mountain looked on his other climbs, Tejas recognized that glacial movement had shifted part of the headwall. The lower part had moved away from the upper part.

Tejas had spent most of the time working his way across the crevasses. That had been enough excitement for one day. Now he was faced with a new problem that carried the same consequences. A mistake could mean his life. The bottom of the headwall meant more dangerous steps.

Not being able to find the fixed ropes was a disappointment, but Tejas had anticipated the possibility. When he divided his equipment at 14,000 feet and left some things behind, he had packed plenty of rope to go with him. If there was a time it would be needed, he knew it would be here on the headwall. McKinley regulars know to bring fresh rope with them. They know it's often needed because ropes fray, and it's the guides' way of contributing to the maintenance of the mountain. Tejas would have to tie new rope into the existing rope when he found it above.

The headwall is so steep though—about a fifty-degree angle—that Tejas did not want to climb it without rope and carrying a heavy pack at the same time. So he shrugged off his pack and began to climb, seeking handholds and footholds without a rope's protection.

"I didn't want to climb without some kind of protection," said Tejas. "It gets icy."

Icy indeed. The headwall was completely iced over. Tejas, gingerly lifting one foot after the other, plunging his ice ax into the wall of snow and ice, climbed step by cautious step. He was briefly distracted, but also pleased, to first hear and then see a raven. A sign of life. But he had to concentrate on what he was doing. In an unforgiving environment, in a climb with no room for mistakes, this place on the mountain allowed even less margin for error. One missed step meant one very long fall.

"If you slip and can't self-arrest, due to the fact that it's ice, you could go quite a ways," said Tejas. "You could go five, six hundred feet."

Even if the deep snow slowed the speed of the slide, the momentum would carry a climber back across those crevasses, and quite possibly into one.

Tejas climbed for some distance, then drove into the wall a metal anchor to which he could attach the rope. He hooked his new rope into the anchor, tested its strength, and rappelled back down the face of the wall.

He put his pack back on and climbed the same terrain again, back up his new rope to where it met the fixed rope. Finally, he could move quickly and without serious worry.

"Once I got to the bottom of the fixed line, it was bang, bang, bang, bang all the way up," said Tejas. "It was just a matter of step-by-step rhythm."

When he made it to the top of the fixed ropes, Tejas was at 16,000 feet. As it had almost every other day on the mountain during this climb, McKinley threw something new at him, found some different way to disrupt his plans and make him go more slowly than he anticipated. The sky was darkening. He would not get to 17,200 feet this night. Instead, he would have to camp here, an unpopular camping spot even in spring because it is exposed to the wind. And by now, Tejas had certainly come to respect McKinley's winter winds.

Resigned, Tejas pulled out his shovel and began looking for a good site to dig a new snow trench. A thought occurred to him, and he paused to consider. Where would it be? he asked himself, searching in his memory for any detail that would help. For if he were lucky, he would end the day with much more than a secure place to spend the night.

A few minutes into his digging, the point of his shovel struck something solid. And it wasn't ice. He had uncovered another big cache, a storehouse of food and fuel. He had a feast.

"It was a treasure trove," said Tejas.

For the second time, Tejas had uncovered a buried stash of food when he was running short of his own supplies. A second reward for hard work. This find wasn't pure luck. That detailed knowledge of the mountain and of the habits of busy-season climbers paid off here once more. Tejas thought he knew where such a cache, which was protected in duffle bags with a climber's name on it, could be located.

"It was in a logical place," he said. "I thought I might hit something. And then, 'Bingo!'"

It is against Park Service rules to leave trash and equipment behind on climbs, so Tejas refused to say who the stuff belonged to.

"I'd rather not get other people in trouble," he said. Especially since those other people had been so helpful to him when his stomach was rumbling.

The duffel bags contained a large stack of freeze-dried dinners, such as beef Stroganoff and sweet-and-sour pork—"which was really good." Also, there were so many candy bars and packages of chocolate that it seemed the benevolent climber might have gone trick-or-treating before burying the goodies. There were

Reese's peanut butter cups, Snickers bars, Hershey bars, and more powdered milk than in the Talkeetna grocery store.

Tejas ate two beef Stroganoff dinners and drank a dozen chocolate milks. No Chinese banquet had more courses than Tejas indulged in.

"It was great," he said. "I had all the hot drinks I ever wanted."

There was so much food in the bag Tejas uncovered that he didn't even make a dent in it. The weather remained kind to him, too, as he dug the snow trench and sawed out the large snowblocks to block the wind.

Far away, the sky was fiery orange, a picture-perfect sunset over the snow-capped peaks of the Alaska Range.

Heading Up

Tejas listened for wind, then looked outside. The weather was good.

On this day, Tejas faced one of the most demanding problems of the climb. Between his pleasant camp at 16,000 feet and the next camp at 17,200 feet, where all guided groups in spring and summer stop for a rest before making their one-day assaults on the summit, is a ridge. In summer, thick snowfall blankets the ridge and the comparatively heavy human traffic pounds out a path. There is exposure—steep, open slopes—on both sides, but a careful hiker, moving steadily, is in danger only if the height disconcerts and dizzies him. In summer, the climbers sink into the snow and the snow holds them safely in place.

The parade of climbers is steady, and once thirty or forty people have crossed the ridge, their footprints form a trail of sorts. They make their own steps and create steps for the people coming behind them. Ground that has a steep slope is flattened out.

But in winter, the circumstances are different. There is no herd of people tramping the snow. There is no one at all, and nature takes over. Some of the snow gets blown away, and the snow that sticks hardens, freezes, and turns to ice.

"The mountain you're climbing in the winter is more difficult," said Tejas. "It's harder just because you don't have footsteps all the way. You are making the footsteps. You're breaking trail. You're fighting generally colder weather, and the mountain's steeper."

This was a day that Tejas approached even more cautiously than the others. He broke camp slowly, using the fuel he had stumbled upon to keep the stove going long enough to warm his boots thoroughly.

It was brutally cold—Tejas isn't sure exactly how cold—but he knew he risked frostbitten fingers if he didn't keep his mittens on for all his tasks, and he knew he risked frostbitten toes if he went ahead as planned with one layer less than usual on his feet.

Tejas went to extravagant lengths to get his feet warm before he started. Leaning on his ice ax, he kicked each leg 150 times to get the circulation going. That was good for only so long, but once he started moving on the ridge, he wouldn't even have that luxury.

Clearly remembering the difficulties his crampons had been giving him, Tejas decided he must leave his fat, insulated over-boots in his pack for this stretch of the climb because the heel clamp of the crampons might not adhere to them. Removing one layer meant the covering on his feet was much thinner, but it also meant the crampons were much more likely to stay in place. If a crampon slipped off on the ridge, there was little room for adjustment and maximum danger of a fall.

Once, on another McKinley climb, Tejas's crampons had slipped off. First one, then the other. But it had happened sequentially, a minute apart, not simultaneously, so Tejas had had time to fix one before the next danger confronted him.

Tejas wanted to come home from this trip with all of his limbs, and with all of his fingers and toes intact, but he also wanted to make damn sure he came home. The trade-off he faced this day seemed to be between damage to his toes and tumbling off the mountain for a thousand feet and disappearing into some crevasse.

"You die if you fall, you lose toes if you get frostbite," he said. "What's the choice?"

Tejas babystepped across the ridge.

It took incredible concentration, inch by inch across the frozen snow. All Tejas's senses were tensed. He was acutely aware of his surroundings. The vastness of the Alaska Range spread before him, the coating of slippery ice on the ridge. His feet were getting cooler, colder, going numb. Every twenty or so steps Tejas paused, looked down, and checked the crampons to see if they were still strapped on tightly. They always were. Every time he stopped, though, even if it was just for a moment to drink, his body cooled rapidly. He felt the cold this day, but his plan was working.

By midday, most of the way across, the sun came through the clouds. To relax, to loosen his mind and muscles, Tejas put on the earphones of his Walkman and flipped the radio dial to his favorite station for one of his favorite programs, "Homestead." Knowing it was one of Tejas's favorites, but not realizing he would be listening, Gail called Shonti Elder, host of the program, and asked her whether she could say something on the air about Tejas. Passing messages over the radio is a common form of communication in the Alaska bush, where many people do not have telephones, but it isn't usually done in the big city of Anchorage.

Tejas was listening to songs on the program, and then suddenly, Elder was saying his name.

"Friends of Vernon Tejas," said Elder. "We want you to know that he's okay."

Elder told the friends of Vernon Tejas and the rest of the Anchorage listening audience that he was at 14,000 feet and going for the summit. So word was out. Now not only the few people who had helped Tejas get started, who had helped put him on the mountain, knew what was happening; now everyone knew.

Tejas, tired and nervous this day, was renewed and excited by Elder's message.

"I sighed, 'Oh God,'" he said. "It felt so good to know that word was getting out. I knew that Gail knew I was safe. I knew that all my other friends weren't worried, and that indeed I was doing something up there besides just burrowing in. It felt good to know that."

Curiously, though, the sense of renewal didn't last very long. The words warmed his insides for a bit, but they also shifted Tejas's mental state. He was lonely.

"It gave me a real boost, but it made me real susceptible. All of a sudden I realized I missed all those people back home."

This message made him homesick, made him think about the people he was missing. This wide, rough world of white works on a man's mind, and Tejas had seen it do its stuff before to other climbers on group expeditions, who had steeled themselves, pushed themselves, worked themselves hard, and were interrupted by a radio message from a loved one back home. Their resolve quickly dissipated. All of a sudden they wanted to be home, to get off the mountain. Their minds had broken before their bodies. A friendly message had probed and found a weakness.

Having seen this happen to less determined and experienced climbers, Tejas had made it a policy on his guided climbs to keep radio contact to a minimum. Now, here he was, getting his own message from home, and it triggered something in him.

"I realized it was a double-edged sword," he said. "On the one hand, I felt really elated. On the other hand, I really thought, 'Whoa.' I could feel the strain building. But I was able to deal with it."

He was more able to deal with things at first than he was a little higher on the ridge. Then, a different kind of message broke his concentration.

Tejas worked his way up the ridge, up the mountain, still listening to the radio. Near the top of the ridge is a large protuberance called Washburn's Thumb, a big chunk of rock and snow that a climber has to step around to reach the camp at 17,200 feet. It's named after Bradford Washburn, from his first ascent of the West Buttress route. A song entitled "My Old Man," by Steve Goodman, flowed into Tejas's ears, and the words had a haunting and almost crushing affect on him. His emotions were a jumble anyway, knowing that he was getting closer to the summit, knowing that every time he moved he was courting death. The words of the song seemed to describe Tejas's unfulfilled, distant relationship with his father Phill, who had left home when Tejas was twelve.

Tired, feeling the mental strain, feeling battle fatigue, Tejas lost control of his emotions and began to cry.

What he felt most keenly was the estrangement between him and his father. When he was eighteen, Tejas and his father had had a falling out. As a result, he didn't talk to his father for two years, and then he hadn't talked to him since. Fifteen more years had passed without communication between father and son.

He realized right there, through his exhaustion and tears, that if he fell off this ridge, that if he died, he would die without telling his father he loved him. And now, at this moment, he did love him. He didn't want to die. He wanted to tell his father he loved him. He resolved that if he lived, if he made it back home, he would call his father and tell him how he felt.

When he was a little boy living in the Houston area, Tejas's father would read him adventure stories like *Robinson Crusoe* and *Treasure Island*. He felt close to his father then, and swam for him at the local swim club, but found himself unable to comprehend the situation when his parents split up and his dad left home. He took his father's departure as a rejection of him and he became a rebellious teenager. He clashed with school authorities over wearing jeans with holes in them and over kissing a girl in the hall. Then he refused to go along with a suspension until the police handcuffed him and physically removed him from the building. Eventually, he endured his suspension and returned to school. As a penalty, he had to wear a suit and tie for a year. He did manage to graduate and then set out on the road hitchhiking. He had been on his own more or less ever since, and had had no contact with his father.

So many things went through Tejas's mind. He felt lonely, felt his solitude as the only man on the mountain more sharply at this point than at any other time. He had been climbing for how long now? Since February 16. He couldn't believe it had taken this long.

"Man, it's a long trip in this weather," he told himself.

Nineteen days already. Nineteen days! He chuckled to himself. He had planned on sixteen and figured on riding in the Iditabike, too, the long-distance mountain bike race across Alaska's frozen interior. Jeez—today is March 5. The race started today. Not going to make it this year.

Tejas couldn't believe he wasn't done yet. Couldn't believe he wasn't really close to being finished. The top still beckoned, but then there was the way down, too. The way down had claimed Uemura, had it not?

All Tejas wanted to do was relax, but he couldn't relax. Not for one step. All Tejas wanted to do was go home, but he couldn't do that, either.

"I wanted to be home at that point," he said. "If I had known that it was going to be a month of climbing, I wouldn't have gone. Looking back, though, I'm glad I continued because it means a lot to so many people."

But it didn't feel particularly good that day. It was a day of extreme highs and extreme lows. But it was also a day of climbing progress. And there was this to be said for it all: he had made it across the ridge safely, made it to the high camp. There was no camp beyond this one. Only the summit.

Dramatic Memories

In the summer the camp at 17,200 feet is a crossroads. The area where the camp is located is perhaps as large as a city block, and guided groups going up McKinley stop here to regroup in a huge snow cave that can comfortably hold up to twenty people. This cave is tucked into the corner of a large basin. It's not exactly the Sheraton Anchorage, but at this point in the climb it might feel that cozy to some climbers.

When Tejas reached the cave, he found it filled with snow. He shoveled for two hours to clear out a comfortable spot to settle into, but still, that was a lot easier than digging his own new shelter and cutting up ice blocks to deflect the wind.

If the weather is poor, climbers can camp here, regain lost strength, and wait out the high winds or snow. They can shed some gear and leave it here to be picked up on the way back, because there will be no camping up above. The trip to the summit and back is done in a single long day. Any camping done higher than this will be for an emergency bivouac.

Once in a while, climbers, realizing they have overextended themselves, decide they can't go on. They choose to stay here, sometimes sheepishly spending a long day waiting for the return of other members of their party who are stronger.

Sometimes, weather won't permit anyone to go higher at all and the group must turn back. Sometimes, bodies have found their limits and collapse here from exhaustion. Sometimes, minds have found their limits and collapse here from lack of will to go on. Sometimes. But more often, climbers are positioning themselves for the sprint to the top. They are psyching themselves up, not out. They're in a protected spot and thinking how they've come through the dangerous crevasse areas and can now make it to the summit.

"It's the shoot-for-it camp," said Tejas. "It's more of a point camp. Most people are in a holding pattern."

When Tejas reached the camp at 17,200 feet, he was feeling many emotions simultaneously. He knew this place well, knew how it worked on others' minds. And he was indeed in a somewhat weakened state after his tense climb of the day before. That stretch had demanded so much concentration and presented so much danger that it had toyed with his ability to focus, just as the music and words on the radio had toyed with his psyche.

Tejas definitely needed and wanted rest. His experiment with fewer layers on his feet had produced two results. The crampons had stayed lashed on his boots. That was a success. But the comparative lack of protection had cost him warmth. His toes suffered a touch of frostbite. That wasn't nearly as thrilling.

It was superficial frostbite, not advanced, with the seriously blackened toes that come from prolonged exposure to cold. Three toes on Tejas's left foot, including the big one, and two toes on his right foot, also including the big one, were nipped. They were more numb than painful, waxy and dead to the touch. The flesh had turned slightly white.

Veteran mountain climbers are often threatened with frostbite in their extremities. The toes didn't hurt, but Tejas was slightly disappointed in himself. He felt he had let himself down by not being more aggressive in monitoring his circulation.

"Oh, man, I've dropped my guard," was his first thought.

His toes had gotten colder and colder and colder while he was shoveling at the cave's entrance, and he had ignored the warning signs. A mistake like that could have jeopardized his ability to go on. But a quick evaluation of the damage showed Tejas the frostbite wasn't that severe. He would be able to continue climbing, but he must be more vigilant.

Tejas was eager to spend a day recuperating, but knowing the mountain as he did, he was afraid to waste a clear day. One clear day was all any climbing group sought when it reached this place on the mountain. Often, one clear day was all a group got—and all it needed to make it to the summit and back. If the day dawned nice, with the sun shining, Tejas knew that, tired or not, he would have to use it. There might not be another one.

"The weather could still stop me," he said.

He didn't think it would. He figured he'd get that one day. If not this day, then another one soon enough. He, alone, could wait longer than could a group on a schedule. He was in position now.

"Having gotten this far, I had eliminated a lot of the variables," said Tejas. "All that was left was worrying about how the weather would cooperate."

Not only did he have what he thought was a sufficient amount of food in his pack, he also knew where caches of food had been buried by previous climbing parties. He could dig them up if he had to. And he knew that the Park Service had a large cache at the top of a gully 300 feet away. The cache has food, oxygen, ropes, and medical equipment.

"I knew I could stay three months if I wanted," he said. "That was the other consideration in making the summit, along with the weather. I figured I could stay put a week without digging up caches."

Not that he wanted to stay a week, and certainly not three months. He was feeling a little tougher than he had felt the day before, but he still wanted to go home. This was taking one hell of a long time.

Tejas looked outside the cave in the morning with great anticipation but somewhat mixed feelings. If it was good, he was going. If it was bad, he was resting. It was bad. And for once, he was happy. Up until now all delays had frustrated him. But this time, when Tejas felt strong winds and saw blowing snow, he didn't resent it a bit.

He knew he was going to spend the day indoors replenishing his strength and thinking about other days on the mountain, other days on the summit. He knew well enough what lay ahead, that it was feasible, within his grasp.

It would be a long day doing nothing, but there had been plenty of those. Every time Tejas had climbed this mountain he had done it faster than this. February 16? Unbelievable. Twenty days. Not only had he done it much faster, on one previous climb he had reached this point on the mountain from 14,000 feet in about four hours. It was a different story that time. A very different story.

One reason Tejas knew about the Park Service caches filled with emergency gear was that he'd used them before.

It was in June 1986. Tejas was just completing a guided trip and was hanging out at base camp on the Kahiltna Glacier with his climbers. They were waiting their turn to be picked up by a bush pilot and flown back to Talkeetna. The next several hours, though, wouldn't involve an easy flight to Talkeetna. They would be some of the most dramatic of Tejas's life.

The code of mountaineering calls for a fit climber to stop what he is doing, wherever he is on the mountain, and come to the aid or rescue of an injured or sick climber. Sometimes this can cost the fit climber his only chance at the summit, but matters of life and death, or matters that seem to be of life and death, take precedence. After all, the summit will always be there. One can return and try again. It is the responsibility of the fit climber to respond to emergencies.

Tejas was relaxing with his group when two South Koreans stumbled into the camp. They seemed both exhausted and excited, but they didn't speak English. Their behavior didn't seem to be the simple exhilaration of having conquered the peak. Things didn't seem quite right. They were too animated and tense.

"My experience has shown me that means that something's afoot," said Tejas. "We asked them if they wanted some water. They just chugged it, so I realized they'd been moving for a long time. They each drank a quart. We asked them if they wanted food. They stuffed it in their mouths."

This communication was not accomplished through direct question and answer. The only English coming out of the Koreans' mouths between inhaling the food and water was "yes" and "no," and Tejas and his companions didn't know what those affirmatives and negatives referred to.

"We were saying, 'Problem?' " said Tejas. "We were trying to ask, 'Where are you coming from?' "

Eventually, Tejas coaxed out of them the information that they had come from the Cassin Ridge, on the other side of the mountain. The Koreans drew pictures of the mountain in the snow and tried to describe their route.

"Then they made human figures up toward the top and they kept on pointing and saying stuff that I couldn't understand. I couldn't understand the words, that is, but I could understand the meaning."

Tejas took the meaning to be that there were two more climbers from the Korean group stuck high on the mountain.

What he was just learning, since he had only arrived at base camp a short while before, was what base camp manager Mary Palmer had been trying to decipher for two days. She had been monitoring garbled radio signals from near the summit. It was clear that something was wrong, but no one was able to tell exactly what. Ultimately, Palmer taped one of the radio messages and located an interpreter who spoke Korean. When he tuned in on the radio from Talkeetna, she played what was presumed to be a call for help. It turned out that the Koreans, with accents so thick no one could understand them, were actually saying "S.O.S." In English.

Immediately two Park Service rangers, Bob Seibert and Roger Robinson, began looking for volunteers to put together a team of the fittest and most able mountaineers on the mountain and in Talkeetna. They planned to rush them to the top as quickly as medically possible. Acclimatization would be everything in this kind of situation. A man could be the world's strongest climber, but that didn't mean he could just run right up to 20,000 feet. If he did, he would risk cerebral edema, the affliction that hits most climbers if they go too high too fast. The disease can strike quickly, filling the brain with fluid, and kill a climber within a day if he doesn't move to a lower altitude. What the rangers didn't need was a whole new crop of sick mountaineers. The last thing they wanted to have to do was rescue the rescuers.

Tejas's only experience with severe altitude sickness had been while skiing in California, but there is always some form of minor altitude distress if one climbs high.

"Generally, you have a headache," he said. "Loss of appetite, some shortness of breath."

Those are all symptoms, but it is the degree to which they are suffered that matters. Anyone trapped high on a mountain and not moving would clearly be showing much more severe signs of illness.

Austrians Wolfgang Wippler and Arthur Haid, Australian Gary Scott, and American Peter Downing of Denver joined the team. Tejas didn't know Wippler, but he knew that his team was a strong one on the mountain. Tejas had spoken to Scott a few days earlier.

Some of the climbers on this makeshift international team were among the strongest in the world at the time. Scott had just made a remarkable ascent of McKinley on the West Buttress route in less than a day. However, there was one problem: Wippler and some of the others had been up virtually all of the night before in Talkeetna, celebrating their ascent of the mountain. They were exhausted.

The rangers asked Tejas to join the team. Tejas's advantage was that he was the strongest climber who had been high on the mountain most recently. He would need no adjustment to altitude.

"I was free from responsibility since my group was at base camp," said Tejas. "We guides have a responsibility to our own climbers first, but we're also obligated to help the Park Service out when they have rescues."

The Park Service plan was to fly the crack team of mountaineers up to 19,000 feet in a helicopter, find the two Koreans, load them on the helicopter, and fly them to a hospital.

"The idea was to put us in as high as possible, to get 'em as quick as possible, and get the hell out," said Tejas.

The helicopter left Talkeetna about five A.M. One thing the rescuers had going for them was the long hours of daylight available at that time of year. It was near the summer solstice, and this far north the peak period of light meant nearly twenty-four hours of daylight.

One problem arose immediately. Mount McKinley was not in a cooperative mood. At 19,000 feet the wind was blasting. The helicopter couldn't come close to a set-down. Not only that, but the clouds were so thick the rescuers couldn't see anything. They didn't really have any idea where the Koreans were, except somewhere near the summit on the Cassin Ridge. They were looking for a tent, but they didn't see one.

The helicopter slowly worked its way down the mountain. The pilot looked for a place to land at 17,000 feet. No dice. Again the winds were too powerful. Finally, the copter put down at 14,000 feet, just below the headwall, and disgorged the climbers. The Koreans were somewhere in the clouds, about 6,000 vertical feet above them.

Tejas, Scott, and Wippler joined together to make an all-out push for the summit. Haid and Downing served as backup. The trio of tough climbers quickly scaled the West Buttress headwall, much faster than Tejas could ever do it with a group of clients who were amateur climbers. They advanced beyond 15,000 feet, beyond 16,000 feet, to the camp at 17,200 feet.

But the swift ascent was taking a toll. Scott felt the early warning signs of cerebral edema, or altitude sickness. He had to retreat, moving back down to 14,000 feet, or risk serious illness. If he got sick, he too might have to be rescued.

The lead group was now down to two. Tejas went to the emergency cache left by the Park Service and pulled out a 600-foot length of rope and an oxygen bottle. Tejas tossed the rope into his pack and Wippler carried the oxygen. But at Denali Pass, at 18,200 feet, the wind was ripping into the climbers, fighting them as hard as they were fighting the altitude. Wippler, who had slept only two hours the night before, craved rest.

"It was pretty nasty," said Tejas. "And I'd never gone up that fast before. Wippler felt he couldn't go on. He knew he needed some sleep and wisely chose to rest at Denali Pass."

Until that moment, there had been little time to think. The experienced mountaineers had been working fast, climbing fast, believing they could save the two stranded men.

"Up to that point I was thinking *rescue,*" said Tejas. "Here we've got a group of good, qualified mountaineers. We're going to see if we can find these guys and bring them down alive."

Suddenly, Tejas was alone. Still, he didn't worry about that very much. He figured Scott was a very tough climber and would soon rejoin him and that Wippler would rest and catch up, too. What Tejas did know was that there were two men somewhere ahead who needed him. He kept climbing.

Tejas climbed to about 19,600 feet, at a spot on McKinley that climbers have nicknamed the Football Field because it is a long, flat, open area. It was there he realized that no one else was coming. He had worked hard to climb swiftly. He'd told the others, "I'm going to go ahead and I'm sure you guys will catch up to me." Now it hit him that they weren't going to make it in time.

"Little did I know that I was the most acclimated," said Tejas. "There wasn't anybody else up there, and it was approaching midnight as I was going across the Football Field."

Tejas grew emotional. Tears began streaming down his face and freezing in his beard. He didn't know what he was getting into here. He thought that at best there was a fifty-fifty chance he would find people alive. In all his years of rescue work he had never brought anyone out alive. Only people in body bags.

"Your emotions run wild," he said of the situation. "You're pushing your envelope of sanity."

The day had begun at five A.M., but by the time the helicopter dropped the rescuers off and they started climbing, it was about noon. So Tejas had been scrambling upward for twelve hours. He had packed light, carrying only emergency gear that he might need, plus the equipment necessary for his own needs. This included bottles filled with water to keep himself hydrated and food enough for a couple of meals, because there was no way of knowing how long this rescue would take—and there was always the chance the weather would turn and trap him on the mountain.

"I took a couple of lunches with me just so I knew I had plenty of food," said Tejas. "Just in case I got stranded at the summit."

After twelve hours of climbing, preceded by seven hours of preparation and flying, and that preceded by weeks on the mountain guiding a group, Tejas was tired. The weariness seeped into his muscles, and took over his mind. It had all been a rush, and now that he was slowing down, he had time to think.

"Going across the Football Field was where it hit me that I was all alone," said Tejas.

Climbing with this purpose, a rescue, and not knowing what

he would find played on his thoughts. He might come upon two dead men, frozen stiff in their tent. He might come upon two desperate men, totally disoriented, beyond help.

"There could have been two bodies on the other side," said Tejas. "It was very, very emotionally tough, a tough thing to do— to just keep plugging along knowing that people weren't coming up behind me."

Three years earlier, Tejas had climbed up here carrying the ashes of his then-girlfriend, Merilee Engelke, and scattered them to the wind. Tejas and Engelke had traveled around the world together in 1984. She was with him when Tejas first thought of shaving his head. They met some Buddhist monks with shaven heads. That gave him the idea, and he thought about it for some time before clipping his hair off. It didn't hurt that he was going bald, anyway. He added his own twist by leaving the slender ponytail in back as a further statement of individuality.

"There's nothing in my life that requires me to look normal," joked Tejas.

The trip with Merilee was cut short when she became ill. They returned to Alaska. Suffering from an infection resulting from the kidney transplant medication she was taking, Engelke checked into a hospital in Seattle after a twenty-eight-hour round-the-world flight. But without warning, an aneurism burst in an artery and killed her.

Tejas had shared much with this woman, in the outdoors, in other countries. He had said good-bye to her on this mountain, not far from here; being the sole rescuer here now, worn out, fearing that he would come upon death a few steps away, turned his emotions inside out.

"I was emotionally exhausted, physically wrung out, and it was weighing on my mind that there was death all around me," said Tejas. "It was hard to keep plugging away at it and not feel that. It was coming out. I was pretty blue at that moment, thinking, 'God, I hope they're not dead.' That's why I had to keep plugging away, because if I had turned back then, I felt, they'd have been as good as dead. If I hadn't done my best, they would be dead.

"It was almost as if Merilee were right there, at the summit. It was just like I was getting a lot of . . . support. I found myself remembering my shortcomings in my relationship with her. I suppose the connection was life and death, but to fail with these guys would have been to fail with her, too. I had to go look for them. It was real important that I continue."

The fight began here. The body was tired but could go on. The mind might have been more tired still and *didn't* want to go on. So many things were working at cross-purposes with the rescue mission, including Tejas's sense of self-preservation and his normal, cautious approach to climbing.

"Here I was, solo on the mountain in a situation that I'd told people not to go solo on," he said.

The wind was blowing about twenty miles an hour, clouds were drifting in and filling up the sky. It felt like storm weather.

"It didn't look good," said Tejas. "But I said, 'Well, I'm going to go till I shouldn't go any farther, till it is no longer reasonable to keep on going. I still had reserves in my body, so I decided to go at least up to the ridge and look down."

The Cassin Ridge is just over the summit from the West Buttress side. It is a different route up the mountain, a much harder one, and the climbers who attempt it are usually more experienced than those who climb the West Buttress. The guiding groups who lead expeditions of citizen climbers up Mount McKinley don't lead groups up the Cassin Ridge.

Tejas knew, though, that from the summit, or near it from the West Buttress summit ridge, he would be able to look over the edge of the mountain down the Cassin and spot the Koreans if they were still alive, still camped nearby.

"If you can't find them from on top and you can't find them from the air, you can just assume they got blown off," he said.

From what Tejas knew, the Koreans had to be suffering from altitude sickness. He was told they had moved up the mountain in just five days—way too fast to acclimate. Regardless of how strong the climbers were, it would have been better if they had taken at least nine days. All McKinley climbing literature warns people not to go too fast.

Having fought his inner struggle and won, having rested himself a little and been rejuvenated, Tejas set out from the Football Field to the summit ridge. The ridge is about 300 yards shy of McKinley's true summit, or 100 feet of vertical gain, so Tejas was between 19,700 feet and 20,000 feet high for the rescue. He stopped short of the summit itself and peered off the ridge toward the Cassin side.

The view is generally of a bunch of rocks, and when Tejas looked down, that's what he saw—a bunch of rocks and nothing else. He didn't see anybody, so he began making noise. He mixed yelling and yodeling. Yodeling is something of a Tejas trademark in the hills. Sometimes he does it for fun. He says he would prefer to sing but rarely remembers the words to songs, so yodeling is a substitute. It is also in the tradition of the American cowboy, and that pleases him. Sometimes yodeling can be an important signature for communication. Tejas has been in snowy, cloudy conditions when visibility was limited and found that his climbing partner could pinpoint his whereabouts from a yodel, whose sound will occasionally travel well when a yell won't. Tejas tried both this time, hoping that if anyone was there, if anyone was tucked in those rocks or beneath a snowy overhang, he would be heard, and there would be a response.

He got the response he was hoping for. He heard a man yelling back, speaking Korean, or at least he guessed it was Korean. He knew it was an Asian language, anyway.

Tejas was elated. He had been feeling logy, perhaps from lack of oxygen, but the fact that people were alive, that he wasn't just going to be shipping two men out in body bags, revived him.

For the first time in a couple of hours he was anxious to talk on his radio. There had been periodic checks by the rangers earlier, flying around the mountain in a plane piloted by Lowell Thomas. They were perfunctory checks, really. "How are you doing up there, Vern?" Tejas had told them he was the only rescuer left, the only one still going. For the previous two hours, though, when he had been battling his inner feelings, determining that he could and should go on, he had refused to answer radio calls. He thought the rangers might order him back. He was shaky, but at that point he wasn't sure he was ready to abandon the attempt. He didn't want someone else to decide; he wanted to do that himself.

"They already sensed it was bad," said Tejas. "If I had told them that one guy was going up to rescue two guys . . . That doesn't make a whole lot of sense."

He had warned the rangers that he might not call back soon,

but the rangers were starting to worry about Tejas anyway. It had been a long time since they'd heard his voice. There were practical reasons as well as emotional ones for that as well.

"Two reasons I wasn't talking back: it was ruining my concentration, and I was risking frostbite every time I'd get the radio out," he said. "I wanted to say, 'Okay, guys, unless it's real important, I'm just going to go. I'm not going to have the energy to stop every twenty minutes and chat. I've got to get to the top and see what's going on.'"

Once he heard the Korean's voice, though, Tejas whipped out the radio. He had something to report. This way the rangers would know the Koreans were alive and where they were. If Tejas himself slipped and fell, even died, they would know others were alive and still in need of rescue.

"They were relieved to hear from me," said Tejas. "I said, 'I'm going strong,' which was the truth of it. Emotionally, I was a little shook, but it was such an uplift to know I was not going to find bodies, that I wasn't going to go up there and open a tent full of dead guys."

He made his report brief and, renewed, began working. He tapped a couple of pickets into the snow and then tied in 600 feet of rope. Tejas hooked himself to the rope and began rappelling over the ridge slowly, hoping the voice that had called back to him was coming from a spot fairly close to the top. Tejas figured the Koreans would be packing up their gear, anxious for his arrival. But when he climbed down onto the Cassin Ridge, he once more became unsure what to expect. It turned out the Koreans' tent was more than 600 feet from the summit, so Tejas had to drop off the end of the rope and scramble down.

Tejas found two Koreans in the tent awaiting rescue. One, whose name Tejas later learned was Seoung Kwon Chung, was fairly alert. The other, Jong Kwan Lee, was not in very good shape. He was stretched out in the tent, woozy, moving slowly, clearly suffering from altitude sickness. Seoung spoke English but was in such a fog, was so weary, that Tejas couldn't understand what he was saying. And the two Koreans were debilitated enough by the altitude, exhaustion, fear, and the language barrier that they didn't understand immediately that Tejas was there to help them get off the mountain alive.

Tejas gave the men his water, the rest of his food, and a drug to combat the altitude sickness. Tejas took some medication himself, since he had just speed-climbed from 14,000 to almost 20,000 feet in half a day.

"I was a little concerned that maybe I wasn't thinking straight, and I wanted to make sure I was fit for the descent," said Tejas.

That was his next problem. He had to communicate to the Koreans not only that he was there to rescue them, but that he was it. Just him. There was no posse at the other end of the rope on the summit ridge prepared to haul them up. There were no reinforcements. It was just the three of them.

Tejas recognized this as a formidable difficulty. For one thing, the Koreans had been stuck in this spot for about five days. If they hadn't hauled themselves to the top yet, there was nothing to suggest they could do it now, even with help. And help came in the form of one man who wasn't exactly fresh.

What Tejas did have going for him was an improvement in the Koreans' morale. Just seeing him seemingly drop down from the sky, they knew that their radio calls had paid off, that there were people out there who cared and who were trying to rescue them. Plus, water and food had freshened them up some. They should have regained some of their strength and will, Tejas reasoned.

"Seeing me lifted their spirits," he said. "I figured they could get to the top. In some ways, they might not have known how close they were. The depth can be really deceptive. But having seen me just come down from there, they had an idea that yeah, indeed, it was attainable."

Tejas had already made the determination that it was safer, that there was a better chance of more help reaching them, and it was probably easier to go up over the summit and down the West Buttress, than it was to retreat along the Cassin Ridge.

There was still a communication gap, though. The Koreans just didn't believe—didn't want to believe, probably—that Tejas had come alone. That may have worked in everyone's favor. If Jong, the weaker of the two, had truly understood that Tejas was alone here, he might have become too demoralized to move. He might not have had the will to force himself to start climbing.

"They were fairly sure there were other rescuers on top," said Tejas.

Gear was packed, and Tejas and Jong began to walk, hike, and climb until they reached the end of the rope. Tejas waved it, pointed to it, made it clear Jong must clip into it with his ascender. Seoung would stay and climb after them.

Jong shakily approached the rope. His legs were wobbly, he still seemed woozy, and his fingers didn't work the way he commanded them to. He reached for the rope and tried repeatedly to tie himself into it. Tejas told him again and again not to tie himself in, to use his hand-held ascender to clip onto it.

Tejas was telling Jong he must raise himself the final 600 feet to the top; Jong was telling Tejas he couldn't do it.

"He was tying on to be pulled up," said Tejas. "He was trying to tie this knot and saying, 'Up, up, up,' and I'm saying, 'Climb, climb, climb.' He couldn't do it with his pack. I ended up dragging his pack up, but he was able to do it."

Tejas hoped that at the same time Jong had been growing weak from lack of food and water and too much time at high altitude, he had actually been acclimatizing himself enough to make his rescue possible.

Meanwhile, Seoung, left below, was actually jovial, said Tejas, happy because he was sure they were getting out of there, sure they would survive. Tejas hooked his ascender onto the line first. Finally, Jong did the same, and Tejas, moving slowly, one step at a time, worked his way up the side of the mountain. One push of the ascender, one pull on the rope. Over and over. He coaxed Jong through it, back up the same 600 feet Tejas had just quickly descended.

Tejas's instinct was right. Jong did have it in him. He made it to the top, over the ridge, to the basin adjacent to it. But once there, he seemed stunned by what he saw, because what he saw was nothing. There was no one else. There was no more help.

"When he got to the top, of course, the truth hit him," said Tejas. "This is all you got. What you see is what you got. I think that was a real letdown, because once he got up there—he was definitely fagged from the effort of getting up there—but once he looked around, feeling the way he felt, and looked out to the north summit, which is miles away, and not seeing anybody anywhere, he just lay down. That was the last time I saw him up."

That was not good at all. Tejas had needed plenty of his own strength and patience to guide Jong to the top. He was worried that Jong would give up now, would die right there before Tejas and Seoung could get him to a chopper and to a hospital.

"He stayed conscious, but he was definitely fading," said Tejas, "and since his buddy was holding the rope down below, I was just up there alone with this guy. I thought he was out. He wasn't comatose, but . . ."

Tejas felt a chill, not the usual frigidness of McKinley weather, but an internal chill, a fear that after all of his effort, after all he had tried to do, Jong would die right there anyhow.

"How am I gonna get this guy down?" Tejas asked himself.

He would have to carry him. He and Seoung would just have to carry him. It was the only way. They'd abandon his pack and carry him.

"It didn't look good."

But then, abruptly, it looked a whole lot better.

Tejas walked to the edge of the basin, to the beginning of the route that led down, and there, in the distance, just over the ridge, he could see someone. Coming fast was Wolfgang Wippler, who had revived from his nap and was climbing with oxygen and a sled borrowed from Alaska guide Gary Bocarde and his climbing party at a lower camp.

"I thought, 'Oh, man, the cavalry has arrived,'" said Tejas. "Perfect timing. Any earlier and he would have just been looking at a rope hanging over the edge. Any later and we would have had to wait there while this guy got colder and colder, because I couldn't move him. I was pretty fagged at that point."

Without the timely arrival of Wippler, Tejas said later, he's not sure he could have dragged the Korean to safety.

"It was work," he said of what the two of them had to do. "We had to go uphill at Archdeacon's Tower. We were panting. Doing it alone—phew!—Well, I would have been in trouble. There was about five hours of hard work ahead, and I thought I'd have to do the whole thing."

Tejas and Wippler took off Jong's crampons, bundled him up, loaded him into a sleeping bag, and then laid him on a sled. Then they got him going on some oxygen. As they worked on him, Seoung appeared. He had pulled himself up the rope without help. Now he seemed wiped out.

There was no time to rest, though. It was obvious that if Jong was going to live, he had to be brought down to a lower altitude swiftly. Tejas, Wippler, and Seoung set out quickly, but he was strong enough to help only himself. He could walk, but he wasn't fit enough to help heft a man in a sleeping bag.

Tejas and Wippler used the same 600 feet of rope that Tejas had dropped over to the Cassin Ridge to wrap around the sleeping bag and help lower it down the West Buttress. Seoung was given the assignment of carrying Jong's pack. But after a short while he tied it on the end of the rescue rope.

"As we lowered our patient down on the rope, his body weight counterbalanced the weight of the pack," said Tejas, "so he was actually dragging the pack down with him. It worked great until we hit the flats."

They had reached the Football Field, the large basin at 19,600 feet, and were still a long way from home, a long way from being out of trouble. Tejas ordered Seoung to untie the pack and carry it, but just below the Football Field, where the incline is steep again, he tied it back on, and Tejas and Wippler dragged it behind Jong and his sleeping bag.

They carted him down to Denali Pass, just above 18,000 feet, to the camp of Bocarde's party. There they needed help. They were almost out of energy themselves and were starting to lose concentration.

"I was tired and exhausted, and so was Wolfgang," said Tejas. "I was so low on blood sugar I thought I was going to pass out. We'd drag Jong ten feet and stop and puff and cough."

Tejas and Wippler left Jong with Bocarde's party and scrambled down to the big way station, here at 17,200 feet, to rest. They spent about eight hours conked out, recovering from their effort.

Later that afternoon, Bocarde and his climbers lowered Jong in his sleeping bag to them by rope. By then the wind had subsided sufficiently for a helicopter to land, and Tejas and Wippler, resuming the rescue, helped lift Jong into the chopper. Seoung joined his friend, and the two were flown to Talkeetna.

What happened next was the most exciting part of the rescue for Tejas. After they had walked down to 14,000 feet, the chopper came back and flew Tejas and Wippler directly to Talkeetna. That meant they didn't have to climb down to Kahiltna Glacier.

"Which was great," said Tejas. "I didn't want to go all the way back to base camp. It would have been two long, slog-ass days after doing two pretty hard rescue days."

When Tejas reached Talkeetna, Jong was still there, still bundled up, about to be medivac'd to Providence Hospital in Anchorage. He was out of it, unable to communicate with Tejas.

But Seoung was wide awake and very much aware that Tejas had saved his friend, if not both of them.

He thanked Tejas over and over and then tried to force a tip on him.

"I said, 'No, no I didn't do it for money,'" said Tejas. "He said, 'From my heart.'"

Finally, Tejas accepted some money. "I said, 'Okay, from your heart, it's okay.' I didn't want to insult him. And I could tell he was very thankful that indeed somebody had showed up."

The rescue commanded tremendous attention in Alaska, in the Anchorage newspapers and on television stations. Tejas was widely praised, but he tried to downplay the achievement of sprinting up McKinley and hauling a man over the summit.

"This just turned out to be a big success," said Tejas. "A lot of things could have gone wrong, but everything went right. I don't think of myself as a hero. I was in the right place at the right time. I was acclimatized. I had a responsibility to go."

There was much life and death associated with the camp at 17,200 feet in Tejas's mind. It was not only his old girlfriend Merilee who came to mind, not only the rescue. It was Naomi, too. Lots and lots of thoughts of Uemura.

Whether or not the rescue would succeed, whether or not the things that had to go right would go right, whether or not he would be in the right place at the right time, and whether or not he had a responsibility to go: it could almost be said that the same set of circumstances applied here, right now, on this solo climb of McKinley. Except that Tejas, in all his thinking time here, did not feel he had a responsibility to go. The top was so close it beckoned, as if it were a coquettish girl signaling across a crowded room, but Tejas had his eagerness in check. He would not permit himself to indulge in the fantasy of himself on the summit. Not even now. Not even here.

"No, no," he insisted later. "I was still saying, 'I'm just going to give it the best shot I've got.'"

"There are some people who make up their mind and they go for it. Well, that's not a very healthy mentality for a mountaineer. If you get committed and it turns out to be a bad choice, you end up frostbiting yourself . . . or worse. I try not to commit myself and say, 'I am going to the summit.' I'll say, 'I'll check it out.' It's real tentative. I'll go until everything says not to go, or until I get enough input saying, 'Turn back.'

"Which I didn't. On the seventh, it was calm."

Summit Day

When Tejas woke up, he rolled over and flicked on his radio. He heard the time, something between seven-thirty and eight. Then he listened to the weather report for Anchorage. And while the weather in Anchorage might be as mild as Miami Beach compared with what he was seeing here on Mount McKinley, there were still indicators to note. The weatherman said there would be no wind in Anchorage that day.

"Hmm," Tejas thought to himself, "this might be the day I was looking for."

Tejas pulled on his outer layers of clothes and emerged from his snow shelter. It was something akin to Groundhog Day. If he saw weather he didn't like, he would scurry back into his home and not emerge again for some time. But if the weather was agreeable, he would stay outside and head for the summit.

Tejas wanted this to be the day. He had rested the day before, letting his body and mind recover, and he thought the seventh day of the month might be auspicious.

"The seventh had some significance to me," he said. "Lucky seven. I figured that would be a good day to try for it. So I crawled out fairly early and took a little reading."

It wasn't exactly a beach day, but then, Tejas wasn't going sunbathing, he was headed to the top of a mountain. The sky was obliterated by thick, fluffy clouds, and there was some snow falling. Visibility was about 100 or 150 feet—a minor whiteout. The air was also fairly calm. There was a breeze, but Tejas assessed all the conditions and decided it was "definitely doable. What we're looking for."

On a day like this in the city, a person might not even think of driving to the store without snow tires, might think it would be a good day to call in sick. By the standards of McKinley winter weather, though, Tejas could call it a good day, one to use. He began packing his gear.

It took until 11 A.M. before he was ready. When everything he needed was in his pack, he made himself a meal. Tejas knew he would need all of his strength this day. In the summer, if things go very smoothly, a guided group can make the round trip in ten to twelve hours.

"If you're really good, you can get there in ten hours," said Tejas. "If you're really bad—I've heard of people who take as much as twenty-four hours, which is nasty. Talk about people burning out by the time they get back. People have died on summit day."

Tejas can recite the names of climbers who died on summit day. Some fell. Some overextended themselves.

"One little thing can throw it off," he said. "The weather can change, a crampon can come off. They didn't allow enough margin of safety for something to go wrong. It's happened. Of all the days on a trip, the summit day probably takes the most lives."

Tejas didn't want to be out there for twenty-four hours, and he definitely didn't want to die. But a lot of how long it would take was up to the mountain. The mountain was still the boss.

He began climbing.

There is long, sloping, steep terrain between the camp at 17,200 feet and Denali Pass, about 1,000 feet higher. The climber must traverse the Autobahn here, so called because, as on the West German highway it is named for, some out-of-control speeds are attained. The Autobahn is extremely dangerous because it is usually blown clear of snow, even in summer, and if a climber slips, he slides a long way with little hope of self-arrest.

Getting to the Autobahn wasn't as bad as Tejas thought it might be. In summer, there are footprints to follow and even step in. Those were covered over, buried under feet of fresh snow, but the wands stuck in the snow to mark the trail were still visible. The wands helped show Tejas the way and prevented him from walking off the side of the mountain in the falling snow.

In some ways, navigation became easier the higher Tejas got. He guided himself by old standby landmarks, but beyond that there were many wands left in the trail. Typically, climbers are extra careful about getting lost high up, so they use more wands to mark their steps. If they've still got plenty of wands left, they figure now is the time to use them.

Without the tracks, though, he was slogging through deep snow.

"It was the most difficult climbing I've seen on the upper part," said Tejas.

In summer a climber can sidestep along the top of the Autobahn ridge; now all the snow was gone. The traverse to Denali Pass was nothing but a slick layer of ice. It was so hard Tejas had to stamp his feet to get any crampon point penetration. One misstep could mean one of those nasty, bouncing, high-speed Autobahn rides. One misstep could mean a fall of 1,000 feet, back to below the 17,200 camp, back to where crevasses could swallow a man in their jaws.

"If I were to fall down and be out of control for more than a second, I'd have been out of control for the rest of my short life," said Tejas.

Tejas, nerves atingle, edged his way across without a mishap. His eyes were riveted on the ground and his mind glued to the task. Except for fleeting moments when he thought of Naomi Uemura. Was this where it happened? Did Naomi slip here? Did he catch a crampon on his gaiters? Or did his bunny boots squirm out of his crampon bindings? Is this how he died?

And then Tejas was safe at Denali Pass. He was at 18,200 feet above sea level; 1,000 feet down and 2,000 to go. This was a milestone, another place oh-so-familiar from summer climbs. He was going the right way, on the right path, still heading up.

From the pass, the south summit, or true summit of McKinley, is to the southeast, about two miles away. Tejas certainly couldn't see it. He could see little this day, little of his surroundings, little of what lay in front of him. On a clear day in summer a climber can see the Muldrow Glacier and the tundra stretching away all green. Even with the cold all around, the smell of the freshness of the land wafts over the mountain.

"In a whiteout, you just have to imagine what it's like out there," he said.

Tejas kept going over more rolling terrain. There were some icy patches, worse than in summer, more slippery, but not as bad as on the Autobahn. It was a nice, gradual incline, not too tough, along the West Buttress ridge for about a half mile. He made steady progress, just putting one foot in front of the other. He couldn't see much, couldn't see far, but the snow didn't hinder him much, either.

On past Archdeacon's Tower, named for Archdeacon Hudson Stuck, the organizer of the climbing party that made the first ascent of McKinley in 1913. Tejas passed between Archdeacon's Tower and a rock knob above 19,500 feet, and that brought him to the flat, broad area around 19,600 feet he knew so well. He had reached the Football Field. It was here, for the first time, that he allowed himself the freedom of thought to believe he would make it to the top. Only here, so close to the finish, did he release the governor on his commitment. It was going to happen. The man who had never convinced even himself that he would definitely make it was finally convinced. He, Vernon Tejas, was going to climb Mount McKinley solo in the winter.

"Now it was no longer a maybe," said Tejas. "It was clearly, 'Let's do it.'"

Then reality intervened. Almost as if reading his thoughts, the mountain struck back, as if to say, "It most certainly is still a maybe; it's not over until I say it is."

Perhaps twenty-five feet below the summit ridge, Tejas found himself wading through fresh, deep, snow, the deepest snow he had seen since 11,000 feet—ages ago—and suddenly the snow settled. It dropped, like a buckling floor. Tejas said it made "a whomping noise." The kind of *whomp* that scares the hell out of you.

"It's the snow talking to you," he said. "When the snow is talking to you, you're supposed to listen. You're not walking on concrete."

Tejas froze in place, a statue, scared to take another step. He appraised his location, the snow, and the overall situation, and realized he could be in trouble.

When snow drifts over in windy conditions, it becomes a pack rather than individual flakes. When a pack of snow settles, it means it wasn't firm. The snow might seem firm on the surface, but the texture below it might be unstable. The weight of a man might be just enough pressure to set the snow in motion and turn it into an avalanche. The ground sloped at a thirty- or thirty-five-degree angle.

"Great angle for an avalanche to happen," said Tejas. "Great conditions. You have a lot of really hard, wind-packed snow and ice underneath this pillow. I could go down 500 feet and get really beat up in the process."

Tejas stood still for a few minutes, examining his options. If the snow did give and slide would he be carried away? What were the chances it would? It could be that this was an isolated patch and none of the other snow around him would collapse in the same way. Or was this a warning to get the hell out of there? Before setting out from the Football Field, Tejas had contemplated taking a longer route to his right. He had chosen this one instead.

"What I had to do was decide if the snow was going to go," he said. "My ice ax was saying there was a good, solid base underneath. If the snow went, maybe I could plant my ice ax and hold. But what would happen if the slope came from above me? Well, it would sweep me off like a hand sweeping away a fly. Maybe I just hadn't stepped on the trigger yet."

But another twenty-five feet of walking would take him out of this area, away from the danger zone.

Tejas could backtrack and start again, or he could take his chances. He believed he was only about fifteen minutes from the summit. If he'd retreated, gone back and started all over, it would probably have added about an hour to his climb. Weighed against his twenty-one days on the mountain, that didn't seem like much, and weighed against the risk to his survival, it didn't seem like anything at all. But there was one other thing to consider. It was four P.M. and it was getting dark. If he went back, the darkness might close in and prevent him from getting his summit chance, or cause him grief on the way back down to the camp at 17,200 feet. If he went back, he might be squandering the only chance he was going to get.

Tejas felt very strong. Until he stalled here, he had been moving at a world-class pace. This was actually the fastest he had ever gone to the summit from the high camp.

"I was cooking right along," he said. "I was in good shape. With all the rest I'd had, all the time I'd had to acclimate, I was feeling good."

He chose to keep going across the snow field.

"So it was a gamble," said Tejas. "But it was one I could justify due to the fact that if I got back in the dark, I would be in a pickle. This was one time I felt that I pushed my margin right to the fine line. I guess I called it right. I'm definitely aware I could have just as easily been wrong. Avalanches kill lots of people."

In fact, one of his close friends and climbing partners from Mount Logan, Todd Frankiewicz of Anchorage, was killed a few months later in an avalanche, caught while backcountry skiing.

With an intake of breath, Tejas walked forward through the snow. Nothing happened. No more whomps. When he reached the other side, Tejas's stomach calmed, and his spirits lifted, too. Now he really was going to make it to the top.

The summit ridge of the West Buttress on Mount McKinley begins at 20,000 feet. The climber is heading east as he gains the final 300-plus feet of elevation over perhaps 300 yards. When it is clear, the view from the ridge as he approaches the small summit point is among the most beautiful in the world. The scenery is of the sprawling, white Alaskan Interior with the protruding points of mountaintops angling towards the blue of an arctic sky. But it was not clear. The panoramas of the magazine photographs that lure tourists to the forty-ninth state were not on display. They lay behind a curtain of thick clouds and falling snow.

Tejas knew it was all there, though. He had seen it many times. Just as he knew every step of the summit ridge. It is not a straight walk, or climb, directly to the top.

"The ridge bounces around a little bit," said Tejas. "But it's

125

all known territory at this point. There's one place where you have to walk on the back of a cornice for a ways. It's a huge cornice, about forty feet thick in one spot."

In the days just prior to this, Tejas had become emotional a few times. He had thought of Merilee, of his father, of Uemura, and of life and death. No one could have blamed him if his eyes had filled a little bit here, or if his heart thumped extra hard. But it didn't happen.

Tejas reached the summit at four thirty in the afternoon.

Alone at the top. Alone with his thoughts. They came from every direction, just like the snowflakes hitting his bright red parka. The thoughts rushed through Tejas's mind in a dizzying, fast-forward movie. They came in a torrent, a river of thought, thoughts in fragments spinning past, thoughts big and whole, thoughts tiny and insignificant.

His mind saw what his eyes couldn't. Alaska stretched before him for miles around: the heartland of Alaska, its vast, snow-blanketed, wind-swept Interior, its mountains bold, sculpted, and high. Near mountains, big mountains, forbidding and cold. Distant mountains, deceptive white triangles on the horizon. His mind saw it all, all of Alaska, this frozen land of the Last Frontier. This rugged terrain where no man walked, where no man lived—there he walked, he lived. His mind saw it all, yet his eyes saw nothing but swirling gray clouds, swirling white snow.

The only man in the silence. He walked and lived.

Alone on the roof of North America, Vernon Tejas, just a few days shy of his thirty-fifth birthday, stood staring into the blankness, staring at the birthday present he had given himself, a birthday present he couldn't see. He was alone on the summit of Mount McKinley, 20,320 feet above the sea.

No man had ever scaled the majestic, snowy slopes of the continent's highest mountain alone in the dead of the mean, soulless Alaskan winter—and lived. McKinley had never permitted it, had taught many men stern lessons, bested their spirit, sapped their energy, turned them away. Some had surrendered, some had died, some had done both.

For twenty-one days Vernon Tejas had climbed, fighting through the bitterness of biting wind and blowing snow. He had been trapped, he had been battered. But he had climbed. Twenty-one days! He had made it.

No wonder the thoughts came so fast, so furious. Some of them were happy-to-be-there thoughts. Some of them were I-can't-believe-it thoughts. And there were even some Is-this-all-there-is? thoughts. Finally, he spoke: "Wow!"

He felt a surge of relief, knowing it was downhill from now on. And there were thoughts of Naomi flashing through his head. He'd made it this far. Bits and pieces were flashing through his brain. He had a good feeling: he had chosen a goal for himself, and he'd done it.

Tejas had been here before, but this was different and he wanted to remember the view, what it looked like. But he couldn't see anything. All he could see was the usual whiteness in the sky.

"The summit's not what you're there for," said Tejas. "It's the view."

He could close his eyes and see what he was missing. When it's clear atop Mount McKinley, you can see everything.

"You can see—miles. For me," said Tejas, "it's as if you've seen Alaska, because you've seen the heartland, out to the ocean. You see down the chain, the Aleutian chain. You can see the eastern part of the Alaska Range. You can see way over to Delta. Foraker. That'd be over to the southwest. And of course, Hunter's down there. Looking down the south face of McKinley is exciting. Pretty spectacular."

On this day it wasn't spectacular, it was white.

"You can't tell they're clouds because there's no definition to them," said Tejas. "Everything's white. You can look off the south face, but before you go over the edge of the ridge there, you could be five feet from the ridge and you wouldn't know. You would not know that it drops down eight thousand feet just five feet from where you stand. Visibility is about one hundred feet, but you can't tell it's that far because everything's white on white."

Tejas had made it to the top and wished to savor it. How nice it would have been to stop here, camp here, wait for the clouds to break and see the world from here. And how deadly. The clouds clouded Tejas's sight, but not his mind. The summit did not belong to him. He was merely a visitor, a fleeting visitor, his muscled body protected in a thick parka, his head hidden under his fur-lined hood, his bushy beard coated with ice; that was actually all evidence that he was an intruder. The cold, the white, reached out for him.

With all of the songs he'd heard on his radio, you'd think one would play in his mind for the occasion, but the tune his head played was *It's nearly o-ver . . . I can come down.* It was his own song of relief.

Tejas's elation was controlled elation, mixed somewhat with pensiveness. "I was feeling elated that indeed I had—knock on wood—navigated it successfully," he said.

He thought of Merilee, too, and her spirit living with him here. "It was just a feeling of missing her. It was important."

It was also important to prove in some way that he had been there. One of Tejas's prominent thoughts was, "I hope these photos come out."

Some of the earliest climbs of McKinley were later proven to be hoaxes. Solo climbs preclude bringing along witnesses, so evidence in lieu of verbal reports must suffice to show the climb has really been made. People don't spend much time on the summit point of McKinley because of the exposure, but they do leave strange things behind to mark their visit. Cans of beer have been buried there; women's underwear, too.

Tejas had a camera to snap pictures of himself on the summit. He had also brought things to leave at the summit as proof of his ascent. One of those things was very serious and the other was very silly.

Tejas took very solemnly his feeling of responsibility to plant a small Japanese flag on the summit in tribute to Uemura. The Japanese climber had come close to making this same climb a success and sacrificed his life to do it. Here on the summit, Tejas felt a special bond with Uemura and felt it proper to honor him.

"I felt indebted because of the inspiration he had been for me," said Tejas.

But Tejas also generally chooses not to take himself very seriously. So he also planted an empty can of Spam on the summit, too. This was a private Alaskan joke. An Anchorage nightclub called the Fly-by-Night Club has a zany, comedic proprietor

The summit in a whiteout: The can of Spam is an example of Alaskan humor, but the Japanese flag in honor of Naomi Uemura was Tejas's heartfelt memorial to a fallen climber. **Photo by Vernon Tejas.**

named Mr. Whitekeys who writes and stages Alaskan musical comedy revues. His club serves such delicacies as Spam nachos, and his tongue-in-cheek Spam jokes have become a trademark. Tejas snapped a picture of himself, beard frosted over, grinning and holding the can. It was originally going to be a sealed can, but along the way, at one time when his food was running low, Tejas ate the Spam.

"If you're not having fun, you've missed the beat somewhere," said Tejas. "I wanted to make sure that if the flag indeed got blown away, and if anybody were to go up there, they would find the can of Spam and know that I indeed had been there. I was still working with the unknown. At least if I didn't come down alive, I wanted people to know I'd made it."

Tejas managed to snap only a half-dozen pictures before the lens on his camera froze. He did get one closeup of his face, eyes peeking out from under a hood coated thickly with ice.

"It didn't matter anyway," he said. "It was just white on white. The photos I wanted to take as evidence that I'd reached the summit, nobody can tell where they were shot. It's not like the photos they take on the top of Everest, where you've got the Chinese tripod set up behind you. Everybody knows that's the summit because they've seen the Chinese tripod so many times. There wasn't anything like that up there, just a couple of white bamboo wands. And snow."

As happy as he was to have made it, Tejas didn't let his happiness overwhelm him. This is a danger that all climbers face. Usually, they have spent so much time and effort to reach the summit, that they linger there to reward the spirit that has been so strong so far. But on a big mountain, that can be fatal. Often, as in this case, daylight is waning and the descent becomes a race against the clock, a race against being trapped into bivouacing a night in the freezing cold and risking your life. The minutes spent on the summit may be precious, but cutting those minutes short may be more precious still.

Late in the afternoon, as darkness began to descend, Tejas's only companions were his thoughts, thoughts of his home, of family, of loved ones. And then one thought pushed its way through, pushed through the jumble of all the others, reverberated louder than all the others: he must keep walking. To walk was to live.

Tejas spent only twenty minutes on the summit of McKinley at the apex of his historic climb, and when he turned to walk down, turned to retrace his steps, he was very focused. He had to remember there was danger.

"It's the same distance as it was going up," said Tejas. "There's the same exposure to crevasses, to avalanches, to freezing, to hunger, to starvation."

Tejas did not pray. He said he never actually prayed on the climb, but he thought spiritual thoughts, tried to commune with God more than anything. "If there is a Lord," he thought, "make this go good."

With an effort of will Tejas erased the emotion of joy and regained the ability to concentrate.

"I'd done the challenging part," said Tejas. "Now all I had to do was reverse what I'd done. I'd done it enough times in the past. I knew it took only two days to get back down to base camp."

Two days. It had taken twenty-one to get here. Two days to base camp in clean, clear weather conditions. Two days to base camp if Mount McKinley let him. Given the weather he had seen through February and into March, there was no reason to think Mount McKinley would.

He had made a path to take him to the top. Now the icy path before him led down.

Vigilance

As Tejas turned away from the summit, turned away from the place he had spent so much time and energy to reach, and was leaving after such a short while, he thought of only one thing: Get down and get out.

"Go like hell to get down," he said. "Go like hell, but don't trip—you can still get hurt."

The specter of Uemura was never more real. It was known that Uemura had made the summit, and it was known that he disappeared not too far below it. Sometime in the next few hours Tejas would pass the spot where Uemura had made his mistake. Uemura hadn't died hibernating in a snow cave, he believed, Uemura had probably made a misstep and tumbled to his death. Tejas didn't want to find the place. He wanted to understand how it happened, but he didn't want a replay, either.

Tejas cleansed his emotions. He put aside his joy at safely reaching the summit. He quelled any sense of nervousness. He purged his mind of thoughts of home and warmth, then he focused his mind and eyes on his task and began to descend.

It wasn't hard to focus. For one thing, being alone was a constant reminder that there was no one else to count on. Being alone at the summit of McKinley was hanging it out pretty close to the edge of the envelope, as the test pilots say. There was hardly a time during the climb when Tejas didn't feel a tension, a pressure to pay attention to every tiny detail.

"You can't forget to dry your gloves one night, even though it's really an easy task," he said. "Same thing with your socks and booties. It's doing little things, doing everything about 110 percent."

His determination was to behave professionally, prudently, and in a businesslike fashion, the way he had his other fourteen times on McKinley.

He told himself, "I've got a job to do right now."

That job was to get himself back to his shelter at 17,200 feet. That job meant descending 3,000 feet of rugged mountain. It was 3,000 feet of vertical descent back to the safe camp where the snow cave was, where the food was, where he could rest. It was infinity if he was careless.

Although climbing up a mountain is a lot more of a physical strain than climbing down is, a descent can be more dangerous because the actual steps are different.

Part of it is limb-eye coordination. Climbing upward, the hands lead the way and they are right in front of the face. Where you go is right in front of the eyes. Going down, the feet go first, and they are farther away. Plus, the method of stepping is different. Going up, the climber rests all of his weight on his toes and the front points of a crampon. Going down, all of the weight must balance on the heels. The full brunt of the weight on snow or ice might break away a hunk and knock the climber down, and once it is going down, a body picks up momentum.

"A fall is hard to arrest," said Tejas.

He moved swiftly, stepping cautiously but confidently over terrain he had visited many times before. It took only an hour to drop 2,000 feet to Denali Pass. But then, that wasn't the hard part. There was nothing coming off the ridge to worry him. The real travail still lay ahead. Ahead was the Autobahn.

If the Autobahn is dangerous on the way up, then it might as well be a war zone on the way down. Even if the footing and weather conditions are precisely the same, even if both cooperate, it is still far more dangerous because the climber's condition is not the same. The climber is weary. The climber is cold. The climber is likely to be emotional, either depressed over failure to reach the top, or elated over his success. In either case, he may not be as sharp mentally. If he has failed to make the summit, his mind may be clouded over with self-doubt, the kind of distress a rejected lover may feel. If he has succeeded, he may face a letdown, a loss of concentration, thinking the hard part is over and it's all downhill from here. It can be, too—much too swiftly from a fall.

"I psyched myself up for the Autobahn because I know it's the place you get hurt," said Tejas.

It's not the same kind of psyching a halftime pep talk from Knute Rockne saying, "Win one for the Gipper," will bring. Tejas psyched himself up using the starkest of terms.

"You say to yourself, 'One slip here and you could die,' " he said. "That gets your attention. Same thing I do with my clients: 'Wake up, guys, this is dangerous.' "

Tejas tells his climber clients horror stories, about how some of the best American climbers have fallen here, been injured, and had to be rescued. Never mind the probability that Uemura died here.

"If his crampons came off any other place it wouldn't have been fatal," said Tejas. "And my crampons weren't doing all that well."

The Autobahn is never a casual stroll. And here, on this day, Tejas was about to traverse it solo, unroped, and it was slicker, icier, than he'd ever seen it.

"I went down the Autobahn very slowly," he said.

He focused on each foot's placement, on whether the crampon points dug in and gripped, and on making sure that when he swung one foot in front of the other, the metal crampons didn't catch on his pants or boots. He crossed one foot over the other on each step and inched downward.

Walking with precision, walking ever-so-slowly, Tejas became more convinced than ever that this was where Uemura erred. On the way down from the summit, it was so easy to fall. He was fatigued. There was little protection, little margin for mistakes. With each crossover step Tejas pictured Uemura. He gripped his ice ax tightly, ready to save himself if he stumbled. Yes, this had to be the place, had to be the way that so seasoned a man as Uemura had died.

"The Autobahn's harder in the winter than in the summer," said Tejas. "Naomi's gear was at 17,000 feet. He'd radioed from the summit, said he'd made it. The only place you can really get hurt is on the Autobahn. About every ten steps I looked down and checked my bindings."

And then Tejas was across. It was over. He had made it safely, almost. There were still a few crevasses, but he managed those in the fading daylight.

When he reached the camp at 17,200 feet in near-darkness, he checked his watch. It was seven P.M. It had taken just three hours to come down 3,000 feet from the summit. It had taken just eight hours round-trip; a fast summit day. And for the first time on this day, Tejas could exhale without thinking about it, could move without thinking about it, could feel free and truly appreciate what he had done. Best of all, though, he was that much closer to base camp, that much closer to going home.

The camp was well stocked, but one thing it didn't have was champagne. That night Tejas celebrated anyway. It was not much of a meal by sea-level standards, but by McKinley standards it was a state dinner. He cooked up a freeze-dried dinner of sweet-and-sour pork and toasted himself with Ovaltine. Cup after cup of Ovaltine. He figured he deserved it.

Telling
the World

At nine A.M. Tejas reached for his radio and made his first attempt to let the world know what he had done. He got on a
general copy, asking aloud repeatedly if anyone could hear him.
He was hoping Lowell would be flying over and he could tell him.
Unknown to Tejas, Thomas had been making regular flyovers,
had tried to reach Tejas on the radio, but hadn't been able to
make contact and had never seen him on the mountain.

The first voice Tejas picked up belonged to a woman named
Ginger at a distant roadhouse on the Parks Highway, the main
road between Anchorage and Fairbanks that runs past the entrance to Denali National Park.

Ginger knew who he was, said Tejas. "She said, 'Oh, you're
the guy . . .' I told her I just made the summit."

Ginger congratulated him. Tejas asked her to patch him
through to Talkeetna. He hoped to connect with Thomas, the
park rangers, or someone from the climbing community.

The woman tried several times and finally it worked. Cliff Hudson, the bush pilot who had flown Lyon in to the Kahiltna Glacier, came on the radio.

"I said, 'Made it,'" said Tejas. "'I'm on my way down. I figure I'll be out in two days. Two days down to base camp.'"

Hudson was the first one in the mountaineering community to know that Tejas had made the summit and was all right. He said, "Great!" and was thinking, "He's a tough son of a gun."

The conversation lasted only a few minutes.

"It was mainly to get the message through that he was okay," said Hudson.

As soon as Tejas signed off, Hudson got on the telephone and called Thomas to let him know Tejas was safe and successful, and alerted him to get ready to go in and meet him on the glacier.

This set off a chain of phone calls. Thomas called the rangers, Seibert and Robinson, and then he called Gail Irvine. She had been without word of Tejas for some time, ever since Robinson's radio contact when Tejas was still on the way up. By this time she didn't know where Tejas was on the mountain, didn't know if he was okay or not. He was long overdue from the time he had told her he'd be home, so although she had faith in his abilities, she was starting to worry a little.

"It's a profound thing for someone to leave and for you not to know if you'll see them again," she said. "There's that element. Still, I was thinking very positively. I tried to give him support."

In his wilderness endeavors, Tejas is frequently out of touch with Gail, so this wasn't particularly unusual. There was just a considerably larger amount of risk involved. Since Irvine couldn't communicate with him directly, she tried to communicate with him spiritually.

"I would just sit and meditate on him several times a day," she said.

As she spoke with Thomas, she quickly grasped the situation. A milestone had been achieved, but Tejas was only half finished.

"I was very happy for Vernon," she said, "but I also remembered that Naomi had died on the way down."

Irvine called some friends and told them Tejas had made it to the summit of Mount McKinley in winter. Soon, friends were telling friends. Word spread through Anchorage.

On the mountain, Tejas felt good. He knew the word would

be out. His friends would know he was still alive and climbing. His friends would know he had done it. He packed up his gear and moved out of the camp at 17,200 feet for the last time on this climb. A short while later, when he had descended to Washburn's Thumb at 16,600 feet, Tejas heard a plane buzzing overhead. Tejas knew it was Thomas from the distinctive sound of his plane. He immediately whipped out the radio and loaded his warm batteries.

The sky was still a shroud of thick white and Tejas couldn't see the plane. It was Thomas, though. He had climbed into his plane and flown to the mountain in hopes of spotting Tejas. On the radio, Tejas tried to direct him to where he was standing.

"I was hoping he could see me," said Tejas. " 'Lookee, I'm here! I'm alive!' I could see him." But Thomas never could see Tejas through the whiteness. The two men talked.

Thomas was thrilled when he heard the news directly from Tejas that he had reached the summit.

"I was just delighted," he said. "Very, very pleased. He was pretty matter-of-fact. I asked him how he was fixed for food and fuel. Then he said he was going to try to get all the way down to twelve thousand or eleven thousand feet," Thomas reported.

Tejas wanted to get way down the mountain by nightfall and then head for base camp on the Kahiltna Glacier the next day. It was a Tuesday; he suggested Thomas plan to come get him on Thursday.

Thomas said that was fine, but oh, one thing Tejas should know. There was a storm headed his way and he should try to make it down even faster if he could do it. Then they signed off.

Thomas did another flyby of McKinley, zooming down low to base camp to see whether Tejas's food cache was visible. It wasn't. It had snowed so much since he had dropped Tejas off that it was completely buried. Thomas realized that Tejas would never find his supplies. It could be dangerous if Tejas fought his way down to base camp expecting to find all kinds of goodies and was faced with an empty cupboard.

So Thomas landed on the glacier and dropped off a fresh cache of food and other supplies and marked it well. Thomas was taking a risk himself in doing this, because the weather was deteriorating fast. He had little visibility and it would soon be snowing hard.

"I had to land downhill," said Thomas, "which is always kind of dangerous. I almost got trapped myself. I put the cache where he'd be sure to see it. The clouds were coming in. I had just a little sliver of an opening. I gave it the gun and barely got out."

Tejas had talked with Thomas at noon. After that he moved swiftly and comfortably downward, retracing his steps much more easily than he could have imagined or counted on doing. There were no problems with crevasses, no problems with icy ridges, no problems on the headwall. Piece of cake, considering the altitude, the snow conditions, the gathering darkness, and his fatigue.

By four-thirty in the afternoon, Tejas had made it to the base of the headwall at 14,000 feet. In comparison with the journey up, he was flying, but in some ways it seemed he was still going slowly. He skirted crevasses extra carefully, and darted through Windy Corner. The clouds were rolling in by then, and he knew he was going to get hit with more bad weather. He could make camp here, at 14,000 feet, or make a run for it. He decided to go, to make it as far down the mountain on this day as he could. Damn, he wanted to go home.

Tejas loaded the gear he had left at 14,000 feet as fast as he could pack. It would probably have been wise to camp, but it seemed possible to travel, so he thought he would try to keep going. He'd been on this frigid mountain long enough.

He made the dash down to 11,000 feet cleanly, trying to keep the sled he was hauling behind him from gathering so much momentum it would run him over. He was barely able to see his way through crevasse fields in the dark. The wands he'd planted in the ground on his way up saved him in the night. They formed the path that took him to his camp at 11,000 feet.

"If I hadn't left them, I would have been up a creek," he said.

It was late at night when Tejas arrived—he isn't sure what time—and he was wiped out. He had dropped 6,000 feet in altitude fast, but that wasn't too unusual. Ordinarily, retreating climbers do try to move quickly. The stormy weather had returned. It was blowing with gale force and snowing with fresh ferocity by the time he set up a camp.

Tejas was so tired he didn't take care to dig his usual snow trench or cut big protective snow blocks. He had left the parasail high up on the mountain, so he had no tarp for a covering, and it seemed too time-consuming to cut so many snow blocks for a roof, too. This was a no-frills camp. Instead of building a whole new house, Tejas dug only a foxhole.

It didn't matter how cold or snowy it was that night, though; he had no trouble falling into a deep sleep.

New Storm Warnings

Alaska awoke to the news that a man had climbed Mount McKinley alone in the winter.

On the front page of the *Anchorage Daily News* a headline read, "Lone climber scales McKinley."

The story by the Associated Press began this way: "Mountaineer Vern Tejas reported by radio Tuesday that he has scaled Mount McKinley. If he descends safely, he will be the first to complete a solo winter climb of North America's highest peak."

Alone on the mountain at 11,000 feet and still quite removed from reports of his achievement and, indeed, from all of civilization, Tejas was contemplating the same thing: "If he descends safely." When he woke up, he realized his quickie, makeshift shelter had been barely adequate.

The wind had blasted all night long, and when he shook himself awake, he found himself under a foot of snow that had blown in on him.

The weather was bad. It was windy, cold, and snowy. The smart thing to have done would have been to stay inside and see whether it would pass. But Tejas was starting to run a little bit short on patience. He had done what he had set out to do and he was more than ready to go home. Not only that, but now he was expected. He had told Lowell to come get him on Thursday, hadn't he?

"I was really motivated to get out," said Tejas, "because I'd told everybody I was going to be out. I wanted to get out of there. It was time to go. Even though that area is pretty protected from the weather, I knew that as soon as I got out of the bowl, I'd be hitting some pretty stiff winds. I said, 'Heck, these are whiteout conditions.'"

Tejas strapped on skis. It was flat enough and snowy enough, and he could make better time. He skied into the full brunt of the storm. He was back in a region of heavy avalanche danger and some crevasse worry. That combination could definitely mean serious problems. Given the way the snow was blowing and drifting, he could ski right into a crevasse without knowing one was there.

That's nearly what happened. He was wearing his aluminum ladder for protection again, though. Tejas figured he could feel his way around the crevasses that had so concerned him on his climb up, but he couldn't see that well. Once, he looked around and realized that although he was standing on a patch of solid snow, thirty to forty feet away there was a gaping hole in the ground. If Tejas had been a little off course, he would have gone right in.

On the other side of the crevasse, the terrain steepened, and Tejas found himself strapped into skis, tied into his ladder, dragging his gear on a sled, and trying to ski uphill with a sixty-mile-an-hour crosswind.

"Not much fun," said Tejas. "Coming out of this crevasse area was the worst time of my whole trip."

Tejas tried a sidestepping technique to get up the hill, but whenever he turned, the sled would slip downhill. His body was getting all twisted on the skis and in the ladder, and forward progress was extremely tough to come by. He wasn't steady on his feet, and the wind pushed him back. Tejas fell down repeatedly, and though the fresh snow softened his landing each time, it was also deep enough for him to sink into. It was hard to pull himself upright.

"I kept slipping, sliding, hitting my knees, getting back up again," said Tejas. "All of this above a known killer crevasse."

The frustration mounted. He was moving so slowly, moving so little, it was almost like running in place.

"This is not a good day," he said.

He should have read the warning signs, he figured, when he woke up in a sleeping bag full of snow. But he hadn't heeded that clue and he'd started out on the trail. He had to keep moving. He couldn't make a camp in the middle of a crevasse field. He couldn't even tell if he was going down the mountain, or up.

"When you're in a snow cocoon," he said, "you can't see up or down. It's really hard."

Eventually, he plucked marking wands from a quiver on his ladder and started throwing them in front of him. He was trying to tell which way he was going.

On one icy stretch he fell twenty or thirty times. It was ludicrous: up and down, up and down. He was getting nowhere at all. Earlier in the trip, Tejas had cracked the outer layer on his double-lens goggles. So now, snow blew into the crack and filled the space between the lenses, blurring his vision.

"I tried several times to face the wind and start moving, but I was just sandblasted," said Tejas. "It was really painful. I could feel ice starting to crystalize in my cheeks."

In the midst of all this, Tejas recognized that he would not get to base camp no matter what he did. His goal shifted from reaching the Kahiltna Glacier to getting someplace to make a camp to hole up in.

"It would've been suicide to push it in this kind of storm," he said.

And one thing Tejas was not, was suicidal. He had proven that over and over again on this climb. He had acted with self-preservation in mind day after day. Now that he was almost through, now that he was almost home, it was not a time to make rash choices and alter his methods. It wasn't worth it, regardless of how much he ached to go home.

"It behooves you to be able to call it quits sometimes," he said.

When he stopped, Tejas had been out in the storm for four

Heavily muffled, Tejas cut blocks of snow to construct yet another snow shelter in the extreme cold of Mount McKinley. **Photo by Vernon Tejas.**

hours. He had descended only 1,000 feet. His new camp was at 10,000 feet, still some 3,000 vertical feet above base camp.

The night before, Tejas hadn't put much energy into building a reliable snow shelter. This time the wind and snow told him he had to build something sturdy. He worked hard cutting ice blocks to deflect the wind, and the trench itself was no foxhole. It was more of an underground bomb shelter. After all, it was to serve much the same purpose—to protect him from what was being dropped on him.

"It was strong," Tejas said of that storm. "It was right up there with any of the storms I'd been in."

When Tejas crawled into his shelter this time, he had little expectation that he would crawl out into sunshine in the morning. This storm looked like it had staying power. That bugged him, not only because of the timing, but because he was convinced the bad weather was localized. He was willing to bet that a few thousand feet up or down on the mountain it was clear.

It would have been easy to think that the mountain was taking revenge on him for his success, but Tejas chuckled at the suggestion.

"I don't think of the mountain that way," he said. "I do occasionally think of the mountain as a strict teacher, but not as a vengeful spirit. I think of the mountain more as a friend than as an enemy."

It wasn't much of a friend this day. Tejas was more right than he wanted to be about the length of the storm. When he went to sleep on this night, he was resigned to the fact he'd probably be spending the next day indoors. What he never considered was the possibility that he'd be staying there long enough to pay rent.

"Where's Vern?"

The frustration was building. Tejas knew that on a good day, a clear day, even a cloudy day without wind, it was only six hours to base camp, only six hours to a food cache and a runway for an airplane. But March 9 had not been a clear day. It was a day so bad—so windy, so snowy, so cold—that he knew he wasn't going anywhere at all.

Tejas loved this mountain, but enough was enough. He wanted out. He was more bugged by the weather's capriciousness now than at any previous time on the climb. Since he began on February 16, he had been pinned down over and over. He had been stuck for days at a stretch. But there had always been some value in being stuck. At least those times he could rest, he could store energy for the climb. He still had the goal of the summit in front of him, and that was motivation enough to keep him fresh. But this was different—he was all done. Let me out! he thought.

But then he caught himself. He was not all done. He was not

all done until he was off the mountain. The mountain was reminding him of this essential truth—that the mountain made the rules.

"I've done what I wanted to do," Tejas said to himself. "I've gotten through most of the major dangers on the way back down. So far I'm going good, but if I get stuck here, I'm just like Naomi. I'm history."

For the entire journey, Tejas had had to rely on reserves of energy. Now he had to rely on his reserves of patience. The smart thing, the only thing to do, was to sit and wait it out again. The day passed slowly.

The next day, Thursday the tenth, it was the same thing. More snow. More wind. No go. Tejas drew his sleeping bag around himself for warmth and spent another emotionally sapping, irritating day in his snow shelter.

Down on the planet Earth, people were starting to wonder. There had been no word from Tejas for over two days. He had reported that he would be at base camp ready to go home on Thursday and he wasn't there. He wasn't there and he hadn't called. The population of the state tensed. Tejas's name was on many lips. People talked about him at work around the coffee machine. Would he make it? Was he all right? Where was he? As more time passed, more people began to worry. The name Uemura was mentioned a lot. People feared the worst for Tejas but hesitated to say it aloud. People who had never met Tejas read their newspapers, watched their television stations, listened to their radios, and worried. Would man beat mountain? Would the mountain allow the climber to leave?

In Anchorage in particular, concern mounted. Anchorage is the hub of Alaska, and its 230,000 people make up nearly half the population of the state. It is also the media center of the state, where Tejas lives, where most of his friends live, and where Gail lives and works.

People who knew Tejas the least well probably worried the most. They knew only the history of the mountain, what had happened to Uemura, and how fearsome a place McKinley can be in winter. Those who knew Tejas well were harder to convince that he might be in dire straits. They respected his climbing skills so greatly and gave him so much credit for being a wise man in the wilderness that they did not believe he was in trouble, did not believe he might have died on the mountain he loved so much.

Harry Johnson, Tejas's boss with Genet Expeditions, has known him since 1977, when both became involved with the Alaska Rescue Group. Johnson was supremely confident that Tejas could do it solo in the winter. Before he left, Tejas had met with Johnson over breakfast to tell his good friend of his plans. Johnson said he never worried about Tejas, either before the climb began or during the period when public concern was at its peak.

"If anyone could do it, Vernon could do it," said Johnson. "Vernon deserved to be the one to do this.

"I didn't have any fear for a couple of reasons. It's not uncommon to get stuck up there. I knew there were caches up there, and I knew he knew where they were. I wasn't fearful that something had happened to him. He's a pretty safe guy."

Johnson even tried to joke about the situation. "I'd like to know when he's down and safe," he said, "so I can start planning the party for him."

Gail Irvine wasn't getting ahead of herself. A party would be nice, she thought, but let's just get Vernon back home first.

Irvine is a marine biologist. When she's not doing fieldwork, she works in an office in downtown Anchorage. The office has a window that faces north, and on clear days she can see the Alaska Range from there, though not McKinley itself. For most of the period that Tejas was on the mountain, she was very busy at work. It was good distraction because it prevented her from dwelling too much on Tejas's health and spending too much time wondering about something she couldn't control. Sometimes, though, she would just stare out in the direction of the mountain, thinking hard about Tejas, not consciously praying for his safety, but thinking good, positive thoughts about him, hoping to reach him in some spiritual way.

When Lowell Thomas flew to base camp on the appointed day and didn't see Tejas, he reported to Irvine. Thomas and Ranger Bob Seibert had said Tejas would almost surely be spotted from the air—if it was clear. But it wasn't clear and he wasn't seen. No sign of him at all.

"I was upset," Gail said. That was the first time Irvine cried over Tejas. For the first time she let her nerves grip her and control her thinking.

"I had had expectations he would be out. When I heard that they hadn't seen him, I was worried," she said. "Waiting, that day and the next, were hard for me. Then I moved back to a position of trust."

By this time, Tejas's climb was all over the news. It had been a relative secret in the beginning, but now all of Irvine's friends and coworkers knew and talked about it with her. Once, a news item talking about how people were hoping and praying that Tejas was all right caught her off guard and she started crying again.

Other friends of Tejas kept up a brave front, especially those who knew the mountain and understood his climbing capabilities. From the start Roger Robinson, the ranger, had been confident that Tejas could make the climb and survive. He said he knew Tejas would be all right as long as he let the weather dictate his movements.

"You've just got to wait out the weather," said Robinson. "Everyone assumed he'd find a food cache up there. It's just a downhill walk. When you're going solo, you just can't go very fast. Vern was real careful. He wouldn't disappear on the way down."

It was hard to tell whether friends just didn't want to believe anything bad had happened to Tejas, or whether they knew the man and his habits so well that they had tremendous faith.

Todd Frankiewicz was one who had faith. Frankiewicz, a close climbing friend of Tejas's who would die in an avalanche later in the year while skiing, was with Tejas as a member of the first party to climb Mount Logan in the winter. At 19,850 feet high, Logan, in Canada's Yukon Territory, is less than 500 feet shorter than McKinley. A group of six Alaskans scaled it in 1986.

Frankiewicz recalled Tejas's phenomenal strength on that climb and insisted he wasn't worried. On the Logan ascent, said Frankiewicz, Tejas actually overcame pneumonia without complaint, keeping up with the group and hauling his share of the gear along the trail.

No, said Frankiewicz, no need to worry about Vern. He's okay. He's probably sitting in a snow cave playing the blues on his harmonica.

Tejas considers himself a spiritual person. Not religious, but spiritual. Sitting there at 10,000 feet, he said there was one thirty-minute period that he could actually feel the intense hopes and fears of his friends coming through to him in his snow cave.

"These waves of energy were coming in," he said.

As it turned out, Frankiewicz was precisely right. Playing the harmonica was one of the things Tejas was doing to pass the time. He was so itchy to head out he had to call on all his common sense and patience to quell the desire to move. When each morning dawned nasty, he could only sigh, lie back in the shelter, and try to stay comfortable.

One other place Tejas had needed his patience was on Logan. In its own way, even though he was with others, the climb of that big mountain—one much less frequently climbed than McKinley—had been the laboratory for the McKinley ascent. It had required terrific practice. The mountain was very high: second to McKinley on the continent. The mountain was very cold: minus-fifty degrees with savage storms carried on high winds lasting several days. And he experimented, devising hand-dug snow shelters to keep the climbers warm.

"That's where the idea really came into its own for me," said Tejas of the winter ascent. "I figured if I could get that high, why couldn't I go five hundred feet higher on McKinley?"

In 1986, Tejas hadn't yet made up his mind to climb McKinley solo in winter, but the Logan climb helped provide the background and confidence that made it possible.

"I wasn't planning on doing McKinley, but I was realizing McKinley was possible," said Tejas. "Logan was an incubator for the idea."

Some of the pride of being part of a group of Alaskans making the Logan climb rubbed off, too, and stuck with Tejas. Cocooning in his latest snow shelter at 10,000 feet on McKinley, Tejas could reinforce his patience and his sense of achievement by recalling the Logan experience.

The men had spent twenty-eight days on Mount Logan, facing down temperatures of fifty below zero and winds that transformed the feeling on the skin to one hundred below zero. When it got to be too much, they dug their snow caves and waited. Often, under stress, in dangerous weather, at high altitude, climbing parties can be ripped asunder by frayed nerves, exhaustion, and tension. This party was remarkably harmonious. It was a happy bunch. When pinned down by heartless weather, the guys played cards, sang songs, or listened to Tejas on his harmonica.

Frequently, climbers emerge from extended expeditions as enemies; the bickering has undone friendships. These climbers were so patient for their goal of the summit, they emerged as friends and partners. There were no injuries or frostbite, never mind deaths. The spirit of the group climb had paralleled the spirit of Tejas's solo climb.

Once back in Anchorage from the Logan ascent, climber Willie Hersman noted that no major problems had arisen. He praised Tejas's style and the soothing effect it had had on the group.

"Vern had a lot of good ideas and we followed them all," said Hersman. "I remember there were times we could have been in trouble, but we were well organized."

The climbers had stood on the summit of Mount Logan on March 16, 1986. It was Tejas's thirty-third birthday.

The party had coped with bad weather on Logan. For some reason, Tejas had figured the weather on McKinley would be less volatile.

"Little did I know . . ." he said.

Now, here he was again on an intimidating mountain, burrowed under the snow, with his thirty-fifth birthday approaching. He did not want to celebrate his birthday by himself, in a snow cave on Mount McKinley.

"I wanted to be home by my birthday," said Tejas. "There were so many things I was missing."

Tejas looked outside the snow shelter. He saw nothing but snow. He was anxious to go, but this was no weather to go in. Patience, he admonished himself for the millionth time. Patience will get you home alive.

Whiteout

Friday night, before he went to sleep, Tejas turned on the radio to listen to his favorite programs. Instead of music he caught another mention of himself. There was a taped interview with Lowell Thomas, and Tejas heard Thomas say he had buried a new cache of food at base camp.

Thomas had sounded chipper, optimistic that no harm had come to Tejas, but later he admitted he was worrying because Tejas hadn't made it to base camp on time. He knew too much history, he was too familiar with McKinley's power not to be worried about a lone climber on the mountain in winter, regardless of his capabilities, said Thomas.

"I always feel responsible when I leave someone there," he said. "I had to worry this time because the weather had been so bad."

Thomas had never radioed Tejas about the new cache of food because he didn't want Tejas to travel lightly, leaving food behind, then make it to base camp and not be able to find the food.

It was too late. Tejas had already done that, more or less. Figuring he'd be at base camp within two days, he had traveled on light rations. He found himself left with French crustacean soup, oatmeal, one candy bar, and Kool-Aid. "Probably enough for two meals if I stretched it," he said. "My variety was limited at that point."

By the morning of Saturday the twelfth, having enough food was starting to become a concern. He could have carried some food from the huge cache on the upper mountain with him, but he'd merely stuck with what he had brought himself. So now he was on short rations, holed up in his snow shelter. The combination of hearing Thomas on the radio and the rumble of his stomach propelled him out the door again.

It was not really a suitable day to hike down. The storm was still blustering, the wind was at full power, and the snow was hitting him sideways, but he decided to go the rest of the way down the mountain.

"I was pretty sure it was localized," said Tejas, "though a storm is a storm. With the motivation provided by running out of food, it was worth risking some superficial frostbite." He laughed. "You have to stop worrying about your handsome looks and think about hypothermia."

Tejas was getting hungry. He couldn't sit at 10,000 feet forever; he'd starve to death. Besides, if the weather on McKinley cleared up, he wanted to be in position to go home right away.

For all his time waiting out the storm, Tejas had accomplished little. This time the storm had waited him out. As he plunged away from the protection of his shelter at ten o'clock in the morning, he plunged into some of the worst weather he had ever braved on the mountain. He didn't know how to gauge the wind velocity, but he did know this: It had the power to knock him down.

"It was enough to stop my forward motion," said Tejas. "I could not look into it."

Tejas hunkered into his parka, awkwardly pulling the hood down on his face with his mittened hands. The wind was whipping his nose and cheeks, and he wanted no portion of his face exposed. As he did that, he had to lean heavily on his ski poles so he wouldn't get blown around.

"And that would happen every other minute," said Tejas. "I'd

153

get blasted for another thirty, forty, sometimes sixty seconds. Then it would lighten up a little bit so I could look around real quick and start skiing like crazy. Then *bam!* It would hit me again."

When a gust came, he would merely cover up and remain stationary. When it ended, he moved on.

It was obvious the mountain, in full fury, was taking its last shot at him. It was as if it had mustered all its forces, all its tricks, to make a final statement, to prevent him from getting away scot-free. It was almost as if it were announcing, "Oh, no you don't."

Tejas ran for it. There was no escape, but he ran for it anyway, against the wind, against the snow, relying on the skills that had taken him this far, relying on his intimate knowledge of the mountain. He skied and stopped, skied and stopped. Finally, he was far enough away from the wind tunnel, close enough in to the protection of the mountain itself, away from Kahiltna Pass at 10,300 feet, that the wind's power slackened.

The softening of the wind didn't mean the skiing was easy; it merely made travel less of a battle. The snow and wind obliterated any semblance of skiable terrain on Ski Hill. There were ruts and gnarls where Tejas didn't expect them. Some of the sastrugi—wind-sculpted snow mounds—stuck up over a foot and obscured his vision of the crevasses beyond. Every hundred yards or so, the wind and terrain conspired to throw Tejas. He was like a punch-drunk boxer—"He's up, he's down; he's up, he's down"—trying to struggle to the end of a fifteen-round fight.

Tejas fell, but at least he was headed down, headed toward base camp. It was rotten outside, but every step brought him closer to the end of the journey. Even every fall brought him closer to the end of the journey. All he had to do was keep picking himself up and he'd go the distance, finish the fight.

He was past 8,000 feet. Near the end. On to 7,000 feet, the tip of the southeast fork of the Kahiltna Glacier, the last stretch before reaching base camp and the runway.

And then he skated right over the crevasse.

He looked down and there it was, right beneath him. He was standing right on a crevasse, skis extended over a two-and-a-half-foot yawning hole in the ground, a hole that he stunningly and abruptly realized was growing. On both sides of him the snow was dropping away, the solid ground was becoming air. Strapped onto skis, hooked into his aluminum ladder, and hauling his gear, Tejas didn't have the freedom of motion for a Carl Lewis long jump, but if officials had been there with a measuring tape, they would surely have been impressed. In a single motion he leaped forward and clear of a crevasse that was big enough to devour him and hide his body forever.

"It looked very, very deep," said Tejas. "It wasn't the crevasse that was so scary, though, it was the fact that I was on one. It was a white field, flat. There was no reason for a crevasse. I stick a pole in and it goes from white to black. All of a sudden this black hole opens up."

The experience left Tejas shuddering. Not only was it a close call, it reminded him that he wasn't finished yet, that the mountain was just as fearsome down low as it was up high. After all, just across the way at this altitude is Point Farine, named for Jacques "Farine" Batkin, who died falling into a crevasse while attempting the first winter ascent in 1967. Tejas should have needed no reminding, but after this incident, he considered himself reminded.

Being able to identify Point Farine, though, was actually somewhat comforting. It meant Tejas was heading in the right direction, that he wasn't off the trail at all.

"The rocks were familar to me. All I had to do was go straight," he said.

Tejas's senses were far keener after this surprise brush with death. This was one of McKinley's nastiest tricks of all. He had not expected crevasses in this area.

"That got me thinking, 'Oh jeez, I could still die yet, even though I'm so close to home,' " he said.

Tejas plodded on, still fighting the storm, now fighting growing darkness, as well as a surprising number of crevasses where past experience showed there usually were no crevasses. He stepped in several more small ones—none so heart-stopping as the first—but he recognized that he was surrounded by them and they weren't all small. Some of the crevasses, he now realized, were as big as mobile homes.

"Big crevasses," said Tejas. "Deep and wide and monstrous. Before I started to go through that, in the whiteout, I just said, 'No, it can't be. It's not worth pushing.' I'd just witnessed that I could be eaten alive."

Reluctantly, he stopped. He was so close to the end. It was perhaps three miles to base camp, but he was going to have to build another camp and quit for the night.

For about an hour Tejas shoveled, digging into the freshly fallen snow, starting to build still another shelter. He was about to start cutting blocks for another wall to deflect the wind when he sat down for a break. As he ate a candy bar, it occurred to him that glacier features were coming into focus some distance ahead. Was it his imagination, or was it clearing?

"I said, 'Whoa, I might make it yet.' "

Rather than resume digging and unpack, Tejas decided once again to go for it. The weather was improving.

"It cleared up enough that I just aced through the crevasses and on down," he said.

When Tejas reached Heartbreak Hill, he was just about at the end of the return trail. When he finally reached what he thought was the spot on the glacier where he'd left his tent buried, it was ten P.M. Tejas had been going for twelve hours in a nasty snowstorm and at last the storm had blown itself out.

He searched for his cache, which included the tent. He had marked it with six-foot wands, but they weren't visible, obviously buried under the thick and frequent snows that had fallen since he had last been here. Then he spotted the wands from the fresh cache of goodies Thomas had left for him.

Plenty of goodies. There were link sausages, peanuts in the shell, rice dishes, all kinds of stuff. Tejas was so hungry he started eating the sausages still frozen while he cooked the other food. Up high it had been brutally cold, minus-twenty, minus-forty, but here, this night on the glacier, it was probably twenty-five degrees above zero.

Tejas cooked until midnight and ate his fill of the new supplies. Then, comfortable in this relative heat, and tired from his long, treacherous day, he didn't even bother to dig a new snow shelter. He just stretched his sleeping bag out on the glacier and lay down.

As he lay there, looking at the open sky, Tejas was elated. He had done it, climbed McKinley in the winter and lived. He had left this spot almost a month before, climbed to 20,320 feet, and now he was back and safe.

He wasn't in Anchorage yet, but basically, he was home.

Waiting for a Ride

Tejas's wake-up call on the morning of Sunday the thirteenth was the feeling of snowflakes landing softly on his face as he stirred in his sleeping bag. Fresh snow meant fresh clouds. Fresh clouds meant no plane. No plane meant no going home. All of this passed through Tejas's mind in an instant.

Damn! he thought. He convinced himself that it was temporary, that it was getting better out, that the sky would clear. Tejas lay there hoping the sun would burn through the clouds and they would disappear and then the buzz of a plane would be heard in the distance.

After a while, he sighed and climbed out of his bag. It wasn't going to happen. The fog was thick and stationary. He quelled his impatience. After all, even on summer ascents, climbers were often stuck at base camp for a day or two because of weather. History showed one thing at least: The sky always cleared up and the planes always came in. Eventually.

"You always figure you might be there one or two days," said

Tejas. "One or two days—I've never waited more. I was tired. I knew I'd be home soon. I wanted to be home by my birthday."

His birthday was Wednesday.

On this day, Sunday, Tejas was particularly glad Thomas had dropped the new cache for him. He searched some more for his own buried stuff but couldn't find a trace of it. That told him that more than six feet of snow had fallen since he had landed on the mountain back in mid-February.

Tejas did little else but sit around and stare at the sky until one o'clock in the afternoon, and then he faced reality. He wasn't going home this day. No one was going to fly through the soup to pick him up.

With nothing else to do and no place to go, Tejas took his time building what he called a monster shelter. This one could have won ice sculpting contests, it was so sturdy and spacious. It was the Hearst Castle of snow shelters.

"I made it bomb-proof," said Tejas, joking later, "because you never know when a bomb might land on you."

Fallout, more likely. As in snow falling out of the air.

Rummaging around in the supply cache Thomas had left for him, Tejas discovered a copy of a week-old Anchorage Sunday newspaper. It was the first newspaper he'd seen in a month, and he was more than mildly interested to see an article in the paper about his climb and the early challenge of Lyon. He spent the rest of the day relaxing and catching up on the news. He read everything from the comics to the editorial page. He even read the want ads.

When he went to sleep Sunday night, having spent the day eating, lazing around, and reading the newspaper—a reasonable approximation of a Sunday for a stay-at-home person in the city—Tejas was sure he'd be pulling out the next day, leaving McKinley behind.

He woke up with that optimistic outlook Monday and kept it as he scrutinized the sky. He could see Mount Foraker, the nearby peak, which stands more than 17,000 feet high and is the second-tallest mountain in the Alaska Range. But the clouds came and went, like a fuzzy TV picture, sometimes ruining the visibility and sometimes parting long enough for a fleet of 747s to land. But he heard no plane, saw no plane.

As much to help pass the time as to sleep in comfort, Tejas built lux-ury accommodations for his last snow shelter. **Photo by Lowell Thomas, Jr.**

The vagaries of weather had turned the ascent into a test of patience; now they prevented Tejas from leaving the mountain. At least at base camp, while waiting to be picked up and flown home, he could read an old newspaper. **Photo by Vernon Tejas.**

"Monday was the most frustrating day," said Tejas. "I'd crawl around back and forth inside my shelter. I'd hear the airplane when it wasn't there."

He hooked up his radio and tried to contact a pilot, a road-house, a ranger, anybody. Couldn't do it. Instead, he picked up fragments of sentences of people talking about the Iditarod, the nearly 1,100-mile-long sled dog race through Alaska's Interior that had begun some ten days before. He thought he was listening in on a radio conversation between guys at race checkpoints, but he wasn't sure.

"I'd turn on the radio," said Tejas, "and start talking. 'Hey, this is Vernon Tejas. Come and get me.' I realized I was just burning batteries. No one could hear me."

Tejas's heart wanted to believe someone was coming for him, but as he studied the clouds, he knew it was unlikely.

"It was cloudy up above," he said. "I could see across to Mount Foraker, but I couldn't see up. Not good. I knew that, but I still was hoping that somebody was going to try."

It was on this day that Tejas toyed with the idea of skiing out from Mount McKinley by himself.

Talk about your dramatic entrances. Everybody in the state is wondering where Tejas is, waiting to hear if he is dead or alive, and he skis out, how far, sixty miles? Picture Tejas on the side of the road, gear piled at his feet, hitchhiking on the Parks Highway. Just like the old days when he hitchhiked around the country. A motorist stops and asks, "Where you going, buddy?"

Tejas cheerfully says, "Anchorage."

"Where you coming from, buddy?"

Tejas leans back in the seat and says, "You're not going to believe this, but . . ."

Most climbs of Mount McKinley start on the Kahiltna Glacier with a fly-in to this base camp, but it is possible to walk and ski in, too. It's a far larger time commitment, involving extra work and extra risk. In his solo winter attempt, Dave Johnston approached the mountain on foot instead of flying in to the glacier.

Tejas was anxious to move, and besides, who knew how long this current blot-out of the sky would continue? Sure, it usually cleared in a day or two, but it could also be like this for a much longer period. If it stayed a long enough time, Tejas could sit there watching his food supply dwindle again.

"If I waited for two weeks, I'd really be starved, and I wouldn't be able to make it," said Tejas. "If I went while I still had a little food, I might be able to pull it off. But there are some nasty crevasses."

Actually, Tejas would never have skied all the way to the highway. He would have skied to an isolated cabin in the area and bopped in on friends. That would have been some image, too—knocking on someone's door, announcing that he's just dropped in for a cup of coffee, and, Oh by the way, can you alert the Park Service that I'm alive?

In the end, Tejas exercised only his mind, not his legs, and decided to do nothing for a little while longer.

"I figured I'd wait, give the weather a chance," said Tejas.

One more night on the mountain. McKinley just wouldn't let go. He went to sleep absolutely, positively certain it would be the last night. It had to be. He had to go home Tuesday. He just couldn't picture spending his birthday lying on the glacier drinking hot water and waiting. He'd waited long enough.

Rendezvous and Return

Tejas stirred at five-thirty in the morning, but it was too dark to tell what kind of day it was going to be. He rolled over and went back to sleep. When he woke up at seven A.M., there was reason for Tejas to be encouraged. He could see the sun on Mount Foraker. He could see clear sky to the east.

Tejas really hoped Thomas would come to get him this day because he was down to a day-and-a-half's worth of food. He'd have to consider skiing out if the plane didn't land. When the sun was fully up and it was clear all around, Tejas realized he would be going home this day.

Even though there was no radio contact, he ran around packing up all his gear and leftover supplies and breaking down the ladder. A frenzied excitement seized him. He double-checked all his packing and cleaned up the area. He was ready to go long before there was any hint of a plane coming into the neighborhood. It was long enough for him to get edgy about whether Lowell Thomas would really get in there. He eventually got a grip on himself and talked himself into relaxing.

"Eat. Be cool. Wait." That's what he told himself.

Shortly after ten o'clock Tejas heard it. Yes, this was it. He could hear the Helio-Courier's engines as it approached the glacier.

Up above, Thomas, who hadn't heard from Tejas for days, was scanning the huge expanse of white beneath him. His eyes were sharp and trained for this kind of search from the sky. Tejas knew what spot to be in, knew the layout of the glacier; if all had gone well, Tejas would be there. Mount McKinley's weather had quit blowing, howling and snowing long enough for him to fly, and that meant it had quit long enough for Tejas to walk to base camp—if he was healthy and able.

As he cruised toward the glacier, a flight he had made thousands of times before, Thomas anxiously looked for a sign of his friend. Finally, he saw something contrasting with the whiteness.

"I could see a little black dot," said Thomas.

At that point he didn't positively know it was Tejas, but there was nobody else on the mountain and it was unlikely a dark spot would be a cache of gear. All that would be buried under fresh snow.

"I let out a 'Whoopie!' in the plane," said Thomas. "It couldn't have been anything but Vern."

Rather than swoop right down to the landing area, Thomas got on the radio and hailed Tejas. It was a very matter-of-fact conversation for two rather excited people.

"How you doing?" asked Thomas.

"Oh, real good," replied Tejas. "How are things going up there?"

Tejas remembers the talk as being nonchalant. "He came right back with, 'How are things down there?' It was so good to hear him. I was joyous. My heart was pounding—I was getting out of there."

And then Tejas's heart stopped. Thomas told Tejas he had to make radio contact with the rangers in Talkeetna and he'd be right back. Instead of landing, he actually flew past the airstrip and away from McKinley, around Mount Hunter and out of view, to make that radio call. Tejas later thought part of the purpose of the call was to tip off the news media that he had made it, that he was all right. But at that moment he couldn't think about anything except leaving. He felt like Thomas's fly-by was a tease.

"He was out of sight, out of earshot, I couldn't hear him anymore," said Tejas. "I thought, 'Please come back. Please come back. Don't do that to me.'"

While Thomas was gone, Tejas motivated himself to make neat stacks of his gear so that he'd be ready to load it onto the plane as soon as his ride returned. But he worked distractedly. His mind was on the plane and his ear was listening for the noise. His only thoughts were on how soon he'd hear that engine buzzing again.

"And then within three minutes he was back," said Tejas. "It wasn't that big a deal. Well, five minutes. But oh, man . . . I'd been waiting to hear that sound for a week."

On this pass, Thomas pulled back on the throttle and brought the small plane to a smooth landing about a hundred yards from Tejas's campsite. Tejas wanted to run to the plane, jump in and fly away, but again he forced himself to be calmer. When Thomas climbed out of the plane smiling, Tejas yelled, "Good morning!" and waved.

Be cool, be calm, Tejas told himself. Lowell is here. The weather is good. You're really going.

"So I walked over to the plane. He walked to meet me halfway. Big handshake. Warm smiles. He was exuberant, and I was probably bubbly. One reason was the success, but mainly it was that everything had worked out and I was safe." The two men embraced in their bulky parkas.

Thomas said, "Sure glad you're down."

"I'm glad to see you," replied Tejas. It was the understatement of his life.

Even with the snatches of occasional radio reports he'd caught, Tejas little comprehended just how much attention he'd received, and he really didn't understand just how much concern friends and even strangers had exhibited over his fate. When he hugged Thomas, though, he sensed some of the emotion coming through.

"I think he was real concerned about me," said Tejas. "I felt that. He wanted to make sure I got out of there in one piece."

Now that he was there, though, Thomas, who had more of a grasp of the way the outside world was reacting to Tejas than Tejas did, wouldn't let him clamber into the plane immediately. Thomas insisted on taking pictures. He posed Tejas with his aluminum ladder, with his gear, and with the plane. Tejas was itchy, but Thomas was low-key about the departure.

A break in the cloud cover finally let Lowell Thomas, Jr., land on the Kahiltna Glacier. But before airlifting the impatient climber home, Thomas insisted on a photo session to help document the historic climb. **Photo by Lowell Thomas, Jr.**

"We've got to take a few pictures," said Thomas. "There's been a lot of interest in this. We better take a few pictures."

Thomas quizzed Tejas about his snow shelters and Tejas brought him over to the final one he built and even provided a short course on how to build one.

"There was no rush at that point," said Thomas.

Not for Thomas, maybe. He hadn't been on the mountain for a month. Thomas was taking things slowly on purpose, though.

He knew that the rangers and Tejas's friends in Talkeetna, a climbing town if ever there was one, were hurriedly pulling together a little party for him. Tejas thought they were going to fly straight to Anchorage—he wanted to go straight to Anchorage—but Thomas quietly suggested that they'd better stop in Talkeetna first.

"Is it all right if we stop and get some fuel?" Thomas asked. "Some guys from the press want to talk to you, too."

As Thomas turned on the radio in the plane, it began crackling with messages for Tejas. A pilot from a passing jetliner radioed congratulations. A woman on the Federal Aviation Administration frequency sent congratulations. A guy in a cabin beneath them in the wilderness with a citizens band radio said, "Nice going."

If they could have seen Tejas, they would have laughed. The plane was so jam-packed with equipment that in the front passenger seat he had to sit with his head stuck between the rungs of his ladder.

Thomas picked up the mike and called Talkeetna. "I have Vern and we're coming in," he said.

Pam Robinson, on the receiving end of the call at Talkeetna Air Taxi, Thomas's office, said, "We'll have a little reception for him."

When they landed, Tejas stepped out of the plane into a crowd of some twenty close friends. He was surrounded by climbers he knew, like Dave Johnston of the first winter ascent party, Rangers Robinson and Seibert, and bush pilots like Cliff Hudson, who had first picked up Tejas's radio signal reporting his success in reaching the summit. Thomas watched and shook his head as Tejas plunged into their midst, happy but controlled, proud but not boastful.

"He was calm, relaxed, had a low-key attitude about it," said Thomas. "That's very admirable."

Tejas hugged everyone he could reach. "It was just so good to grab people again after a month of being by myself," he said.

Johnston thrust into his hands a half-gallon of milk and a banana, then hoisted him off the ground in a bear hug. There was some significance to what might have seemed like an odd food presentation by Johnston. He and the others on the first winter McKinley climb had been given up for dead before being flown off the mountain. When they returned to civilization, the first things he was given to eat were milk and a banana. Tejas understood the meaning of Johnston's little gift.

And then, not five minutes after he landed, Tejas was paged. He was told there was a phone call from Washington and he thought, "Wow, hey, the president's on the phone."

Not quite. It was a phone call from National Public Radio in Washington, D.C., asking for a quick interview, asking him to tell how he did it.

As he went to the phone, Seibert thrust a Dove bar into his hand. When asked how he was doing, he said, "Fine. I'm eating ice cream."

For the first time, said Tejas, for the very first time since he had planned the climb, made the summit, and made it down to familiar territory, it occurred to him that someone besides friends, family, and climbers might care that he had climbed Mount McKinley alone in the winter.

"So all of a sudden," he said, "I realized, 'Hey, this is bigger than I thought it was going to be.' I realized that my success was important to others, and that made me feel good. This was a big thing for me, but to have it mean something for others was truly gratifying."

After Thomas had radioed to her from the mountain following his first pass over the glacier, Pam Robinson telephoned Gail at work in Anchorage to tell her Tejas was safe.

"He's coming," said Robinson. "He's at base camp. Lowell's picking him up."

When Gail hung up the phone and told her coworkers—half a dozen other women—everyone was near tears.

After a short stay in Talkeetna, Thomas bundled Tejas into the plane again and they flew into Anchorage. There the reception was rowdier. There were signs reading, "Welcome Back," and "Congratulations!"

Gail was there and Tejas grabbed her, hugged her and spun her around. And newspaper and broadcast reporters flooded the area, snapping Tejas's picture, firing questions at him, and sticking microphones in his face. Tejas had a press conference going.

"I was at the limit of my abilities," he said. "Skillwise, strength-wise, foodwise, mentally, emotionally—I was at my limit."

Someone observed that Tejas was home in time to celebrate his birthday and asked if that's why he came off the mountain that day.

"Sure, wouldn't you?" said Tejas. "If you had a birthday coming up, would you like to celebrate it in a snow cave?"

Tejas couldn't believe the attention he was receiving. For so long he had been by himself, with only himself to talk to, and suddenly he was in the middle of a mob, the center of attention in a mob.

"It was just too much," he said.

Tejas was happy to be home, happy to have Gail on his arm, happy not to be fighting the wind, happy not to be taking dangerous steps. Happy, too, not to be freezing in temperatures of twenty below.

When someone asked, "Were you ever cold?" Tejas was stupefied. He blinked and laughed to himself. Was he ever cold? When *wasn't* he cold?

"I was always cold," he said out loud. "I'm cold right now."

The reporters all laughed with him.

Still cold, but warming up fast. Mount McKinley, with its fearsome weather and terrible disposition, was in the distance. Tonight, for sure, he would be warm.

The Reluctant Celebrity

Vernon Tejas had departed for Mount McKinley as an unknown. He returned to sea level as a celebrity. On one of his first nights back in civilization, he and Gail attended a St. Patrick's Day dance at the Anchorage Sheraton Hotel and heard 300 people sing "Happy Birthday" to him. So much for solitude.

Reaction to his success was immediate and, to Tejas, stunning. He was instantly mobbed by the Alaskan press. That he expected. But the calls came in from the national media as well. National magazines were calling, wanting to tell his story.

The Alaska State Chamber of Commerce had him to lunch. Elementary schools asked him to speak to pupils. The Rotary Club wanted a slide show. When he made a dinner reservation for himself and Gail at a fancy downtown restaurant, he found a bottle of champagne waiting by the table.

Those were the formal things, the organized things. The informal meetings, the accidental encounters, were even more astonishing to Tejas. With his distinctive features broadcast all over the newspapers and television screens, Tejas was easy to recognize, but still, he had no inkling that his accomplishment would produce such varied and strong reactions in people. Stranger after stranger—people of all ages—approached him in the street, at the grocery store, at the gas station, to clap him on the back, shake his hand, tell him what a great thing he had done. Tejas estimated that in the first weeks after he came home he was approached by strangers bearing congratulations seven to ten times a day.

"It seems to have affected grade-school children, bankers, and ladies in Safeway," said Tejas. "It seems that one of my personal goals in life turned out to be a metaphor for other people's private goals. I never expected a tenth of the reaction I got."

Bob Seibert is probably one of the keenest students of public involvement with Mount McKinley. Seibert, who had been rooting for Tejas, said he understood the public hubbub. The success touched people, he said. "McKinley is such an important part of so many Alaskans' lives."

If Tejas had ever doubted that before, he didn't anymore. "It's the biggest thing around, whether you're a climber or not," he said. "It's the wildest part of the wildest state. It's Denali, the Great One. Everyone else can see that, too. It's Alaska."

One group of people Tejas did expect reaction from was his fellow climbers. As much as it is a special mountain for the general public in Alaska, McKinley means even more to American climbers, especially Alaskans. It is their mountain in the sense that it is their home mountain. It is the big peak in their country, on their continent, the mountain that attracts the international climbing community to their turf.

The solo winter ascent of McKinley was a challenge that had thwarted them. The hideous winter weather had daunted and discouraged and defeated them. Now the challenge had been surmounted. For many in the local climbing world, particularly those who knew and had climbed with Tejas, there was satisfaction in seeing an Alaskan's success, as well as considerable respect for the accomplishment.

Seibert himself said success on McKinley in winter could have been managed by only a talented and confident climber. He called the climb "an astronomical achievement."

Bradford Washburn, the former director of the Museum of Science in Boston, who was part of the pioneer first ascent of the West Buttress in the summer of 1951, congratulated Tejas. Washburn, a pioneer on several other mountains in Alaska as well, greatly admired Tejas's climb.

"The man of steel," Washburn called Tejas. "He had the necessary luck, but he knew what he was doing. He was patient and he had a lot of guts. It requires fortitude and knowing how to climb, how to keep yourself from freezing. I don't care how good you are, that's dangerous. Anyone who wanders around alone on the Kahiltna Glacier has got to be damned good. The ladder was a very smart move. He's a smart guy."

Jim Hale, Tejas's old climbing buddy, said the right man made the summit. "It's neat that an Alaskan mountaineer is able to do that," he said. "I was real happy for him. There are times when that mountain is just plain unforgiving."

McKinley has tempted Hale in winter, but never to the point of making a summit attempt. McKinley in winter seemed just too cold. "It's an awful place," said Hale. "I had thoughts of doing it off and on over the years when I was guiding. There's no question but that it's a whole new level of extremes.

"I think there's something about Denali that surprises people. They can't fathom how cold it is, even in summer. Some of the best climbers in the world have just snuck by. The awesomeness of it is in terms of dealing with the weather. He did it in the way I thought he would do it. He just stuck to it."

Hale said he never worried about Tejas when people were raising the question of a possible disappearance in a crevasse. "I felt very assured," he said. "He was very capable. He was able to pull it off."

Harry Johnson said he, too, had considered trying to climb Mount McKinley in the winter: for about ten seconds. He then quickly dismissed the idea as preposterous.

"That's the last thing in the world I would want to do," said Johnson. "I don't think it would be fun. I don't mind putting myself through challenges, but I want to enjoy life. Living on Mount McKinley for a month at minus-forty degrees doesn't seem like fun."

Tejas, he said, was sufficiently prepared, with experience and capability on high mountains and in extreme cold, to exercise appropriate judgment about when to try moving and when to sit tight.

"When you're by yourself, you can't let your mind wander at the wrong time," said Johnson.

Johnson told Tejas that he had displayed a true talent for building suspense. He joked that getting pinned down and losing contact for a few days made for terrific public relations.

The drama probably did increase public awareness and feeling. "Part of it was the ending," said Tejas. "It happened the same way with Naomi. I'm sure a lot of people thought I went over the edge."

No one, of course, knows what McKinley can throw at a climber better than the members of the first winter ascent party of 1967. Roger Robinson calculated that the heavy snows, violent storms, and subzero temperatures that Tejas faced likely matched the extreme conditions that inspired Art Davidson to title his book *Minus 148*.

"His bad weather was probably the equivalent of what the original ascent party had up high," said Robinson. "He had a reasonable summit day."

Davidson, who knew Tejas before the climb, said the way Tejas handled himself on the mountain is what impressed him. "The beauty of the climb, which was overlooked, is in the meticulous, careful planning," said Davidson. "It's in analyzing every danger and how he was going to get around it. He was like a craftsman, an artisan, refining every little detail. When to push, when to hold back—that's the guts of it.

"If another guy just charged up and made it, he might have lost some fingers and toes. That's what I appreciate about in how Vern did it. He did it with style."

Tejas was gratified by the reactions. With the exception of a fair bit of attention focused on him because of the Korean rescue in 1986, he'd never experienced this sort of acclaim. He both reeled from it and savored it. It was such a new experience to walk down the street and have people ask for autographs, or say hello, or "Nice going." Day after day the accolades poured in, leaving Tejas shaking his head.

"I thought I might be recognized in climbing circles," he said of the praise he was getting, "but it's gone beyond climbing. It's gone beyond the outdoors set. I'm eating it up, though. I'm enjoying it."

One of Tejas's public appearances seemed to transcend the other more intimate, small-group formats. Nearly a month after his return from the mountain, Tejas was invited to give a lecture and slide show at the University of Alaska, Anchorage. The first to admit he is not a smooth public speaker, Tejas faced the additional worry of putting together enough slides to make a show. For $3 a head he had to give the people something besides his smiling face and bald head glistening under the lights. The frozen lens on his camera had prevented him from snapping many pictures, but he managed to pull together enough vistas of the mountain and shots of himself on the mountain from previous climbs, plus some from Aconcagua, to entertain the audience.

Sitting in a university cafeteria as the time for his talk drew near, Tejas admitted to being slightly nervous. This was a new role for him. Still, he figured the crowd would consist mostly of local climbers and outdoorsmen and that he'd know a good percentage of the people.

Not quite. When Tejas walked down the corridor to enter the spacious room for his talk, he was shocked. From a distance, he could see that the room, which held some 500 people, was packed, and the line to get in stretched not only all the way down the hall the other way, but wound up the staircase to the floor above. The organizers of the lecture were beginning to turn people away. Finally, one of them took Tejas aside and asked if he would mind doing a second show.

Tejas was led to the front of the room, where friend and fellow guide Mike Howerton introduced him. Before Tejas could start his talk, the crowd rose spontaneously and gave him a standing ovation. Grinning widely, but blushing furiously, Tejas was speechless. Not a good condition to be in for a guy supposed to be making a speech.

When the crowd quieted sufficiently for him to be heard, Tejas said, "Shucks." Then he took a deep breath. "I'm a little flabbergasted by the turnout. I have a feeling this is going to be harder than climbing the mountain."

Several times in that first month back, as Tejas was inundated with invitations, he made statements like that. He said he'd rather climb McKinley alone in winter again than speak to a large group of people; that he'd rather climb the mountain again than write about his experiences.

But with practice, actually, Tejas was turning into a folksy, reasonably polished speaker. He still couldn't bring himself to brag about what he did, so more often than not he couched the tale of his most desperate and harrowing moments in light humor. At other times, he spoke with great emotion as he sought to convey what goes through a man's mind when he is trapped beneath the snow in the midst of a winter storm like those that had trapped him so many times on McKinley.

"One of the feelings I had up there," said Tejas, "was a feeling that many people's spirits had joined me in the snow cave. I think this made a great impression on me. I'm not a very religious person, but I felt a lot of love coming to me."

Listening to the radio and hearing himself talked about was a treat, said Tejas, and the way the people of the state embraced him on his return was particularly special.

"I didn't realize my climbing would go beyond the climbing community and touch so many people in Alaska," he said. "This has been the greatest reward from the climb."

There was another reward from the climb, too. In a sense, his life's work was validated in the public eye. He had always had respect as a reliable guide, a strong climber, and one who nearly always brought his clients safely to the summit and back. But it seemed that to gain renown in the climbing world, one needed to do something spectacular.

By climbing Mount McKinley alone in winter, by being amply recognized and appreciated for it, Tejas had not only gained in stature, he had gained in confidence.

Another important thing happened after Tejas returned home. He followed through on the emotional pledge to himself to re-establish contact with his father. Tejas picked up the phone and dialed his father in Texas—and got no answer. But his father responded to the message. When Phill Hansel called back, the two men exchanged their first words in fifteen years. His father had read about him in the newspaper.

"We're real proud of you," Hansel said.

So the climb had been a catalyst for changing his relationship with his father. But had it changed anything else in Tejas's life?

For a man locked away for a month in the great white, fighting raging winds and storms, testing his will, his discipline, his endurance, his brains, and skills, for that man to triumph and walk away with no damage: well, that man will surely have learned something of himself.

For a man to celebrate his thirty-fifth birthday the day after emerging from this great white: well, that man will surely take a moment for reflection. Tejas reflected and proclaimed himself the same old Vern. Then he reflected some more.

"It's like someone who wins the New York State Lottery," said Tejas. "They say, 'I'm the same person.' Sure, you're the same person. You have the same social security number, the same fingerprints, the same body, and the same head of hair (in some cases). But when the world sees you differently . . . If everyone had reacted, 'Oh, well, so what?' I wouldn't be feeling quite so self-assured."

But the world hadn't said, "So what?" The world told Vernon Tejas he had done something very special indeed.

Tragedy

In the last days of April, Tejas was scurrying around Anchorage, running errands in preparation for another climb. He was going back to McKinley on May 1.

This time, Tejas was going to the mountain on assignment. He was back working for Genet Expeditions, ready to lead a group of eager clients on what promised to be the experience of their lifetime. There was nothing to indicate there would be anything different about the climb. There was nothing to indicate that anything would go wrong.

Tejas was going back to the mountain for the first time since the solo. This was his sixteenth trip to McKinley. He was scheduled to lead nine climbers up the West Buttress route. This was the same route that had tried to kill him, tried to swallow him up in its crevasses, tried to smother him in fresh snow and blast him off ridges with strong wind. This time, though, it promised to be warmer, and not nearly so lonely.

"I think the contrast will be amazing," said Tejas before departing.

For one thing, Tejas was sure to have a few new stories to tell sitting around the propane stove as the group cooked dinner.

"I've got a whole new repertoire," he said.

He certainly did. He'd experienced things on this mountain that no one else had. The glow of success hadn't quite worn off yet. For the previous several weeks he'd been almost as busy fulfilling commitments to people who wanted to hear those stories in a formal setting as he had been gathering new equipment for the group.

As he drove around town, stopping in sporting goods stores, climbing stores, hardware stores, trying to find all the gadgets and gizmos, and all the climbing rope he needed for the journey, Tejas reflected on the incredible events of the first four months of the year. He'd already been up Aconcagua, all of its 22,835 feet, three times, and to the summit of McKinley at 20,320 feet. That was a lot of work, a lot of time up high.

He wished he'd had more time to savor the solo climb. Going back to McKinley this way was going back to business as usual. It didn't diminish what he had accomplished, but it blurred the memories for him. After all, it was the same mountain, and it was going to be the same route to the top.

"It hadn't been enough time," said Tejas. "But I was looking forward to it. When you're going back to work you feel productive. You tend to romanticize it, but it's a job."

As he dashed in and out of stores, Tejas was interrupted several times by well-wishers. The congratulations were still coming steadily from people he'd never seen before in his life. There were more handshakes, more way-to-gos. At one store, where he found the climbing rope he needed to replace those frayed and damaged fixed ropes on the headwall, the owner recognized Tejas and told the clerk, "Give Mr. Tejas a good deal on whatever he's buying."

On April 30, Tejas picked up his climbers and drove them out to the Genet Expeditions hut in Talkeetna. In winter Talkeetna is inhabited by just a few hundred people. Temperatures dip as low as minus-fifty degrees. There isn't much excitement. The regulars like to sit around the Fairview Inn, where President Warren Harding visited just after its opening and just before he died. They drink, gaze at the sketch of Ray "Pirate" Genet on the wall, and sometimes discuss the mountain.

In May, though, Talkeetna is a flavorful place. It is 110 driving miles from Anchorage, close enough for day trips. Visitors stop in the little gift shops and, on clear days, take in views of McKinley. But Talkeetna is more than a tourist stop. In spring it's transformed into an international city. Climbers from all over the world check in at the ranger station, pile their gear on lawns, set up tents, and wait their turns for flights to the Kahiltna Glacier and other jumping-off points on the mountain. Almost any language can be overheard while you're walking down the street, and some menus and stores have signs posted in French, Japanese, German, and several other tongues. If an adventurer has trouble believing his expedition is about to become reality, Talkeetna will put him in the right frame of mind for climbing.

Tejas took his band of climbers to the Genet location just outside the center of town. He gave them a welcoming speech and put them through an equipment check. Although it was sunny in Talkeetna, it had been cloudy on the mountain that day, and all of the flights were grounded. Though this group wasn't scheduled to leave until the next day, it was possible there would be a delay, he warned them. But even as Tejas spoke, the weather was clearing on the mountain and the pilots were gearing up to clear the backlog of people clogging Talkeetna's streets. Everyone was going to get in this day after all. Maybe a little late, but with long hours of daylight, the pilots could fly till midnight. They'd all get to base camp.

At various times during his solo climb, Tejas reflected that in many ways what he was doing was easier than what he normally did. He had only himself to worry about. On a guided climb, though, he had myriad responsibilities. He had to be mother hen to everyone. He had to make judgments about others' health and state of mind.

As the group gathered, exchanged names and backgrounds, checked and rechecked its equipment, and settled down for a night's sleep, there was nothing to indicate that this group would be any different from any of the others Tejas had guided on McKinley.

But this climb would turn out differently than any of the other fifteen Tejas visits to McKinley. This would be the first time a Tejas climb on McKinley ended with the death of a climber.

McKinley, it seemed, would exact a form of revenge on Tejas after all. It was almost as if the mountain was announcing, "Yes, I let you go, but that doesn't mean they'll all be free rides." It was as if the mountain was reminding him of its omnipotence.

A thirty-two-year-old Anchorage woman named Lynne Salerno was one of the climbers in Tejas's party. By all accounts, one tough athlete. Probably, as it turned out, too tough for her own good. Although nearly sixty climbers (Park Service records are a little sketchy) have died trying to climb Mount McKinley, in May 1988, Salerno became only the second climber ever to die on a guided climb.

The events unfolded this way:

On May 17, as the group pushed toward the summit, Salerno, who had prepared for her climb by taking mountaineering courses and winter camping classes for three years, seemed exhausted. She sat down on a snowfield with Tejas about 800 feet below the summit.

Tejas, who has made a practice of talking to determined but weakening climbers in gentle tones, said he told Salerno it didn't seem that it would be her day. She was dragging. Salerno resisted. She had worked hard for this moment and the summit seemed within reach. There was not much ground to cover. It was hard to see quitting here. Salerno and Tejas sat and talked for a half-hour. Suddenly Salerno, who had seemed spent, seemed to recover. She stood up, ice ax in hand, and said she wanted to go on. Tejas, surprised at this show of resilience, changed his mind. She looked strong enough to continue and make it to the top.

"I reevaluated my earlier decision," he said. "She was rational in mind. She looked fresh and alert, as good as anybody looks up there."

Salerno, who had had the strength and will to overcome a speech impairment, dyslexia, and childhood ailments, summoned the strength and will to make the summit. She plodded up the final ridge successfully and stood on the top of the highest mountain in North America.

But abruptly, coming down, she weakened and faltered again. She collapsed, and three hours after she had convinced Tejas that she was strong enough to go to the top, she died.

Salerno was such a tough woman that on her final stretch run to the summit she had shocked Tejas. She was moving swifter than she had before she took the rest. It was as if she had been renewed, refreshed by the break.

"It was a tremendous rally," said Tejas. "In retrospect, it's obvious she kicked in the afterburners and was giving it everything she had."

At one point, Tejas even left Salerno to check on two other climbers who had gone on ahead. Salerno continued upward at a steady pace. She took breaks, but that's common high on big mountains. Climbers typically take several breaths for each step when they are at high altitude. When he returned to Salerno, who had kept advancing toward the summit, Tejas said she thanked him for having the confidence in her to let her keep going alone.

Tejas went back and forth between Salerno and his other two climbers. Always Salerno was moving. She was tiring, but climbers often tire near the top. The other climbers reached the summit and turned back, encouraging Salerno with hearty comments as they passed to begin their descent. About twenty-five feet from the top, Salerno didn't appear to notice the summit flag, said Tejas. That concerned him a little bit. A mere ten feet from the summit she stopped and insisted she had to rest. It was only a twenty-second rest, though, and then she pushed herself to the top. She had done it.

Salerno wanted to take some pictures, said Tejas, but he said he'd do it for her. It was then that he noticed her cheek seemed white and frostbitten. She had never complained about being cold and, in fact, a short while before had denied being cold. Tejas grew a little bit more worried.

As they lingered on the summit, the weather, which had been so cooperative, so clear, began to deteriorate. It seemed a storm might be moving in. Tejas knew they must move out quickly and start moving back down to the big camp at 17,200 feet.

Only ten steps into the descent Salerno stumbled and fell to the ground. Tejas helped her up, but after ten more steps her legs went out from under her again. It was clear Salerno's energy was draining quickly, and Tejas felt things were reaching a danger point. There was no help close by and the basics of rescue equipment were nearly 1,800 feet below at the camp.

It would be a long, slow, walk back like this. He was afraid Salerno was showing signs of cerebral edema. They kept moving down the ridge slowly, but Salerno kept falling down. She kept asking to take rests and Tejas said her words came out in childlike babbles. They caught up with the other two climbers, and the four of them stayed together, making it down to the Football Field, back to where Tejas and Salerno had sat and talked before assaulting the summit.

Complicating the situation, the weather worsened steadily. The wind rose and howled at forty miles an hour, and the temperature, as the sun disappeared, fell to minus-twenty-five. It wasn't snowing, but the wind was blowing hard and swirling the snow around them. It was just more of the rotten weather Tejas had lived with for a month during his winter climb. They couldn't see where they were going. It was getting too dangerous to travel, and Salerno was having trouble walking at all on her own.

Tejas started digging one of his snow trenches. He wanted them all to have protection from the weather. Then he turned the digging duties over to one of the other climbers and told them to keep talking to Salerno, to keep her awake and as coherent as possible. They had stripped down to lightweight packs for the summit push, but if they were going to bivouac, they would need some more equipment. At the least he could retrieve a stove to use for melting snow.

As he climbed alone in a storm once again—such familiar circumstances now—Tejas cursed himself for letting Salerno go to the summit. He was angry at himself. But the situation was unprecedented in his experience. He was stunned by the way Salerno had deteriorated, even faster than the weather. He had never seen it happen to a climber like that before. Usually, if climbers were strong enough to make the summit, they were strong enough to keep going for a couple of hours back to camp. It *was* all downhill from there.

"It was like a switch turned off," said Tejas of the suddenness with which Salerno had unraveled.

It took Tejas ninety minutes to climb down to 18,500 feet, get some gear, and climb back to the snow trench. By the time he got there Salerno was dead. He called her name. Nothing. He felt her pulse. Nothing except frozen flesh.

182

The other climbers had performed mouth-to-mouth resuscitation. They had lain on her to provide warmth. Nothing revived her. They left Salerno in the snow trench and, climbing six hours more through the raging wind, Tejas and the other two climbers reached the camp at 17,200 feet and safety.

Friends and family of Salerno later said that childhood illnesses, including measles, had helped deaden her sensitivity to pain and cold. She had worked hard as a child and young adult to overcome the difficulties of learning with dyslexia. She did whatever it took to succeed in school, sometimes investing five hours to do homework that others might have done in a third of the time. She had applied the same standards of hard work to her profession as a physical therapist. They could envision the same kind of determination driving her on the mountain, willing her to the top.

Doctors, family, and friends speculated that Salerno had run herself into the ground because she sought with such determination the victory of the summit, that she had exhausted herself and then became hypothermic. It was impossible to tell because, at her family's request, her body was later placed in a crevasse near the spot of her death.

Tejas was dismayed by what occurred. He had used his judgment, done his best, and seen a climber die—a climber in his charge.

"She ran her tank right to empty," said Tejas. "I didn't know it was empty. I thought she had a reserve."

Only a short few weeks before this climb, Tejas had endured hardships, conquered the wind, the snow, his own fears and doubts, and the slopes of this mean and powerful mountain to do something no one else had ever done.

Now, once more, the mountain was stating that it would set the terms of any climb, that it would determine who would make its summit and go safely home. Once more, Tejas was reminded of the fragility of human life on a mountain such as this.

Mount McKinley still had the power to defeat any man, or woman, seeking to challenge it.

Reprise

Vernon Tejas went back to the mountain again in July, this time in the company of another McKinley pioneer, his friend Art Davidson. In 1967 Davidson, Dave Johnston, and Ray Genet had become the first to climb McKinley in the winter. Davidson had told the story of that climb in his dramatic book, *Minus 148*.

Talk about strands of history meeting on the mountain. Davidson and Tejas were among the few men ever to stand on the summit of Mount McKinley in winter. Now they were going to climb together in summer, for fun.

For Davidson it was an extra special occasion. Tejas may have completed his climb only months before, but Davidson had never climbed McKinley or any other major mountain in the twenty-one years since the winter ascent.

The men had reacted in opposite ways to their triumphs. Tejas had returned from McKinley with his appetite whetted, eager to climb again soon, eagerly searching for new challenges. Davidson had been sated.

On the twentith anniversary of the first group winter ascent of McKinley, Davidson spoke about how the intense climbing experience and his close brush with death on McKinley had changed his outlook.

"Many of my most cherished experiences in the mountains have been private," said Davidson. "In a sense, nothing in my life can compare to McKinley. It's the only time in my life I've ever lain in one place for a week and I really didn't know if I would live or die.

"Our companions gave us up for dead," said Davidson, whose party had split up into the summit group and another group lower on the mountain. "It was a prolonged period of facing death. That has left a permanent effect on my life. Suddenly, you realize there are a lot of things in the world you take for granted. You realize how wonderful it is to be alive, just to walk around, to take a breath, to look at trees."

All three summiters suffered frostbite and were hospitalized, in some cases for weeks. Davidson spent the next two decades as a writer, photographer, lecturer, campaigner for wilderness protection, and businessman, living in a tiny place near Anchorage called Rainbow. But then, at age forty-four, he decided he'd like to go back to McKinley, to visit the mountain again, this time with his nineteen-year-old son Dylan. He told Tejas he'd like to go with him.

"It's really neat to be going together," said Tejas before the climb. "I've got all sorts of questions. He's someone to get information from. We both broke ground, and we've got stories to tell—and lies to swap."

Davidson said it was like revisiting his childhood, and he brought the same kind of nostalgic attitude to the climb. The first time he had trained hard and was driven to make the summit. This time he said it wouldn't bother him if he didn't even make it all the way to the top.

"It's like the fishing hole that you went to as a kid," said Davidson. "Now they've built a road there and there's a McDonald's. You want to see it, but you don't really want to go back. There's some of that."

They went in the middle of the month, the middle of summer, with some paying customers who were excited to have two such famous Alaska mountaineers in the group. They had beautiful weather and a beautiful time.

"There were times I had the sense that we were the only ones up there," said Davidson. "But it was also fun seeing other people. The challenge is still there for everyone who goes up."

McKinley had been so mean to both Davidson and Tejas in winter, but this time it was friendly and welcoming.

"One client brought the book," said Tejas, "and that got Art going. He was reminiscing in spots. As we went up the mountain, he told us a lot of stuff about what they had been doing there. It was fun."

Eight people made the summit on the relaxed journey. Oh, and there was one other benefit for Tejas. He went searching for his cache from the winter solo and found it. Just as the weather had buried it completely from view, summer melting had brought it back into sight: Tejas spotted a wand poking up about six inches.

"I hadn't given up," he said.

Another First

When asked to name the coldest place on earth, many people think of Alaska. Vernon Tejas was able to think of someplace colder—Antarctica. And before 1988 ended he had recorded another mountaineering first, one that in its own way rivaled his McKinley solo for drama, partially because it was so unexpected.

If Tejas had planned and thought of conquering McKinley alone in the winter for years, he had given little thought to a solo of Mount Vinson, at 16,067 feet, the highest peak on the Antarctic continent. For one thing, he had no idea whether he would even be able to visit the area. For another, he did not know Vinson the way he knew McKinley.

But on December 12, 1988, Tejas once again did what no man had done before. On that day he became the first mountaineer to solo Mount Vinson. And he did it in just fourteen hours from base camp to summit and back to base camp.

Standing on this summit, surveying the last continent, Tejas was awed. "I did it," he said to himself. "Wow." Then he chuckled at himself, not only for having a reaction so similar to his McKinley solo but even attempting another solo. "There ain't many people that stupid."

Antarctica has always been shrouded in mystery.

Some 2,000 miles south of the tip of South America, it is inaccessible. With ninety-eight percent of its five million square miles layered in ice almost two miles thick, it is a wasteland. And with temperatures in some regions averaging minus-thirty degrees year-round, it is inhospitable. The only residents, besides penguins, live at scientific research stations.

To those who explore the world's high places, Antarctica has always had one rather elusive lure. Mount Vinson, the highest bump on the eighty-mile-long Vinson Massif in the Sentinel Mountains, 800 miles from the South Pole, has been off-limits for mountaineers until recently.

"I never thought I would get to go unless I was going to guide," said Tejas.

First climbed by a ten-man American expedition in 1966, Vinson was climbed only once more before 1983. That year, American millionaire Dick Bass, in his quest to reach the summit of the world's seven highest continental peaks, focused fresh attention on the mountain.

Then Vinson was thought to be 16,860 feet high, but it has since been remeasured at 16,067 feet. And reclimbed. But not very often.

Antarctica is an open continent, with no national boundaries. The eighteen member nations of the Antarctic Treaty of 1959 pledged to preserve for peaceful purposes the vast open spaces first explored by Norwegian Roald Amundsen in 1911. The signatory countries do not regulate the borders.

Nevertheless, visitors need a permit to fly from another country to Antarctica. The flights originate in Punta Arenas, Chile. Since Bass's climb, only a dozen or so expeditions have made ascents of Mount Vinson.

No one beside Tejas, it seems, considered doing it solo.

Tejas had no thoughts of a Vinson solo when he boarded an ancient DC-4 cargo plane in Chile on November 24, 1988. He went to share a friendly trip to the summit with photographer Frank Fischbeck and real estate agent Keith Kerr, both of Hong Kong.

Tejas had guided the same two men to the summits of Mount McKinley and Aconcagua in previous years. They paid his expenses to Antarctica. It was the only way he could afford to go— private wilderness travel companies charge $18,000 and up for a guided climb of Vinson.

"Before, Antarctica was pretty hypothetical," said Tejas. "Twenty thousand dollars is pretty hypothetical for me."

Fischbeck and Kerr had first written to Tejas a year before and suggested an Antarctica trip. They wrote to him a second time after they heard of his McKinley solo, saying great, *now* they could be led by a celebrity. Would he guide them?

He wrote back and said, "Love to."

On the ten-hour flight from Chile, sharing space with two other small climbing groups, Tejas had time to think. He was about to lead two men on a mountain he had studied but never seen.

He was more worried than he had been starting his twenty-nine-day winter solo of McKinley. He had been on McKinley fourteen times before and carried a map of its ridges, crevasses, and dangers in his head. McKinley he knew. This was the unknown wrapped in horrifying tales of extremes.

"I had a lot of misgivings," said Tejas, who kept them to himself. "I'm used to working in the guide mode. What is known is the terrain and not your people, and in this case it was reversed. There was a little apprehension. How cold is it really going to be? Will I be able to get them through the crevasses?

"Forty below. I was told that's what it was going to be. Forty below's real cold. Not if you're going to go for a hike or walk the dog in it, but it is if you're going to live in it. It's pretty hard to cook. You're always trying to keep your hands and feet warm."

Tejas had read accounts of climbing on Vinson and studied photographs and maps. He had done homework. Part of that research included reading an account of the Bass expedition scaling Vinson in temperatures of thirty below zero and facing winds of sixty miles an hour. Even famed British mountaineer Chris Bonington had been shaken by the weather.

"These have to be the worst conditions I've ever climbed in," he said.

The big, old plane glided toward the Antarctic continent in the evening, but with twenty-four hours of summer daylight Tejas had a clear view of the Vinson Massif. The plane overflew it on the way to a landing a hundred miles to the south on a flat, icy plain at Patriot Hills. This outpost is a fuel depot, not a true airport. In fact, the planes don't land on actual runways. They land on ice, and the landing strip is called a blue ice runway.

Not quite everything was white. Only a few inches of annual snowfall coupled with high winds meant some spots were swept clean of snow. Clearly defined rock poked through.

"Ahhh! This is Antarctica," thought Tejas.

They unloaded their gear and then flew by small plane closer to Vinson itself. Tejas sat in the plane drawing a little sketch map of the land in his notebook. It was a precaution, in case the plane didn't come back to get them and they had to ski the hundred miles to Patriot Hills.

"What if the plane goes down?" Tejas thought. It was important to know the way back to the only place that passed for civilization.

Sitting at base camp at 7,500 feet was like sitting in a rowboat beneath the great walls of a glacier. Men were specks against the great towering peaks of Mount Shinn, Mount Epperly, and Mount Tyree, all to the east. The summit of Vinson lay fourteen miles away.

Both Tejas, whose stomach was queasy, and Fischbeck, who was running a fever, felt sick, so the group lingered at base camp for three days. The other two small climbing groups burst ahead.

On November 28, Tejas's group began its advance in surprisingly benign weather, moving to Camp One at 8,500 feet. There was some sun, and it was warm enough to cook without gloves. That was a treat. Tejas described the climbing and the effort to move up as "real mellow."

Tejas thought back to his winter visit to McKinley. There had never been a day like this. He had always been cold on that climb, and frequent storms and high winds had trapped him in snow caves for days at a time. Here he was in the one place on earth where the weather might be nastier and it was almost balmy.

"I was lucky," he said. "It never got worse than twenty below. You prepare for the worst and hope for the best."

On the twenty-ninth, it was actually three degrees above zero in the tents. Tejas was well now, but not Fischbeck. He had a nagging cough. Tejas, who had whiled away hours playing blues songs when he was pinned down on McKinley, chugged seven miles round-trip to base camp in two hours to pick up the harmonica he had left behind.

Tejas took mental notes of crevasses, of curves in the trail, of inclines. He started thinking, "A guy could do that. A guy could do that. This terrain is not all that unbearable."

And that's when he started thinking solo.

"It was in the making as the climb was taking place," said Tejas. "If you don't know what the climb is, you don't think about flashing it. It grows in your mind only because the situation you're in allows it to."

Climbing to Camp Two, the men passed over few crevasses. Vinson's crevasses seemed very different from McKinley's. The Alaskan Interior is constantly besieged by fresh snows. Crevasses can change overnight. On his McKinley solo Tejas had the extension ladder for protection. On Vinson the climbers were roped, but threading their way up a snow gully, they discovered that shallower snow did not mean safer climbing.

"I was walking along and I heard the snow go hollow," said Tejas. "It was crunch, crunch, crunch, boom, boom, crunch. I wondered, 'Why did it make a different sound there?' I would look back and there'd be a slight depression there. That's scary."

Camp Two gets little sunshine. The mountain walls are like Manhattan skyscrapers blotting out the sun. It was minus-ten degrees and nearly windless. This was Antarctica?

"Day after day it was nice," said Tejas. "We were in a window, a good weather window, no doubt about it."

The other groups barreled to the summit, but Tejas, Fischbeck, and Kerr absorbed the scenery. Sometimes it was so clear they could see the outlines of mountains 200 miles away across the flat plains.

"They say you can see the curvature of the earth there," said Tejas, "but that's an optical illusion. You can see it if you want to see it, I guess."

Hiking to Camp Three at 12,000 feet, Tejas realized how much Vinson reminded him of the West Buttress of McKinley, though McKinley is some 4,000 feet higher. Both climbs feature high altitude, lower air pressure because of polar locations, and potentially life-threatening weather and crevasses. Vinson even has fixed ropes in one spot, not unlike the headwall on the West

Buttress route. Once, the climbers had to get up at four A.M. to rebuild an ice wall worn down by raging wind, as Tejas had had to do on McKinley. Resting at Camp Three, their shortwave radio picked up the BBC and they listened to a John Dunne poetry reading. On McKinley, of course, Tejas had tuned into Alaska Public Radio.

There is one other objective hazard on Vinson that comes between Camp Two and Camp Three, something quite different from McKinley's West Buttress. There is an icefall, an area ripped apart by the stresses of glacial movement. Seracs, or big blocks of ice, can give way with no warning, and when they do, there is little time to run or dive out of the way. The Khombu Icefall on Mount Everest is probably the world's best known icefall, and climbers have died there when big chunks of ice have ripped away and tumbled down on them. The Vinson icefall is about three quarters of a mile long, and climbers know to step lively over that ground.

"It's something to think about," said Tejas, "especially when you're soloing."

Nothing happened when Tejas and the others went through.

They reached the small, flat summit on December 7. Not yet sure he was about to attempt the fastest-ever climb, Tejas joked that this was probably the slowest ascent of Vinson.

On a cold but clear day Tejas and the others stood surveying the last continent.

"It was spectacular in a very stark way," said Tejas. "Everything's in black and white. The rock's black and the snow's white. There's no color. The sky's the only thing you get."

But it was big, wild, and untamed, and in the silence the men could be fooled into believing they were the first humans to stand there.

"There's that feeling you want to claim it in the name of the king of Spain," said Tejas.

The climbers lingered at the summit for ninety minutes, a long time on the roof of a high peak. Tejas left a small Alaskan flag there and broke off a small piece of rock as a gift for his brother. There were no major problems, from the weather or the mountain. Tejas thought, "This is real straightforward."

Then Tejas jumped off the mountain.

Parasailed, actually, down to Camp Three. He had hoped to make a similar descent from McKinley but had been thwarted by the weather. Still frisky, Tejas and Kerr climbed 15,356-foot Mount Shinn the next day from the connecting saddle. Fischbeck rested.

As they descended, they passed a group of Australians headed up, at that point the only other climbers on the mountain. Tejas watched the clock. An hour and a half from Camp Three to Camp Two. Three hours more to Camp One. Into base camp another five and a half hours later.

"I added all that stuff up and figured it was conceivable for someone to make it in a day," he said. A long day. Fourteen to eighteen hours, he estimated.

"Eighteen hours is a pretty exhausting day," said Tejas. "Fourteen hours is a stroll in the park." Not quite a stroll in the park, but perhaps doable.

The following day Tejas rested and thought. Soloing changes the terms of climbing. He knew that well enough. Did he really want to do this? Was it the smart thing to do? Could he really do it? He would see.

It was just after four A.M. when Tejas marched out of camp carrying three quarts of water, cookies, granola bars, and some beef jerky. He had no pack, no tent, and no ropes. It was twenty degrees below zero and clear.

Fischbeck and Kerr asked him where he was going. He told them he was taking a walk, that he'd probably be out most of the day. He didn't tell them he was trying to be the first to solo Vinson because he wasn't sure he could do it and he didn't want to boast of attempting something he couldn't carry out.

"I was going to go as far as I could go," said Tejas.

Feeling light without a bulky pack, Tejas walked swiftly across the hard-packed incline to Camp One, then scrambled safely and easily around crevasses. He figured he'd chat with the Australians at Camp Three, but when he got there at nine A.M. they were all asleep.

It had taken Tejas, Kerr, and Fischbeck more than a week to get that high. It took Tejas alone five hours. He was going so fast he had had to remove his outer clothing but was still sweating heavily.

"I was hauling," he said. "I had stripped down to my long johns. I was fired up. It's not often you get to walk around at altitude without a big pack. Without much weight, once you become acclimated, it becomes a playground."

A little higher, Tejas noticed the sky changing. Menacing clouds were moving in. He paused. For the first time the mountain was turning on him. But he knew the Australians were at Camp Three. That meant he would never be more than a few hours from help high on the mountain, and with his friends in base camp he knew he'd never be more than a few hours from help on the bottom part of the mountain. The biggest danger might actually be on the lower mountain later on, if he walked into a whiteout and got lost. He did not know this mountain the way he knew McKinley. He couldn't feel his way sightlessly through a storm.

Tejas reached the summit about four and a half hours after leaving Camp Three. Over the final hours, in the final miles to the summit, the clouds descended, thick and dark with snow, and blanked out everything. Tejas saw soup, not sky, for most of the time. Until he took the final steps to the top of Mount Vinson. Then the heavens cleared and he saw Antarctica—a white, snowy desert, an empty, frozen land—stretched before him.

It was one thirty P.M. on December 12. Nine months before, Tejas had become the first man to solo Mount McKinley in winter, and now he had become the first man to solo the highest peak at the other end of the world.

Tejas's stay on the summit was brief, perhaps only three minutes. He did look out at the beautiful land, but he looked harder for his Alaskan flag. He scooped it up, for proof. His breath coming hard, sweat soaking his clothing, and with joy in his heart, Tejas ran off the summit as the clouds closed in on him again.

Tejas ran faster than the clouds floated. There was enough visibility for him to see the Australians well below, trekking down. Yelling and yodeling, he saw bewildered climbers look up at the sound, but it seemed they couldn't see him yet. As he descended, still shouting, a couple of them turned around.

"It was as if they were saying, 'Who the hell is that?'" said Tejas.

Who could blame them? They thought they were alone on the mountain. Tejas drank some water and continued his flight.

He jogged down past Camp Three at 12,000 feet, past Camp Two, past Camp One, through a gathering whiteout, and three miles more to base camp at 7,500 feet on the flat plateau that stares into the broad shoulders of the Vinson Massif.

There was one moment of anxiety. The lower mountain was a fog of blowing snow when he reached it. But Tejas never lost the trail, and when he burst in on Fischbeck and Kerr at six P.M., they gaped. Fourteen hours after he had told them he was going for a walk, he came into camp on the run.

"Where have you been?" his friends asked.

"I had to go back and get my flag," he said, waving the tiny Alaskan state flag at them—the same flag they'd seen him plant on the summit of Vinson five days earlier.

"You went back to the summit?" they asked.

In his diary entry that night, Kerr called Tejas "Superstar."

In his own diary, Tejas wrote, "I soloed Vinson today. I'm very tired, but amazed at my reserves. Wasted, but still kicking."

Compared with the McKinley solo, when all of Alaska followed news reports of his progress and feared for his life, Tejas's Vinson solo was accomplished in virtual secrecy. He phoned Gail and told her, and that was about it for a while, because Tejas didn't come right home. He went back to Aconcagua and led another guided climb, and then he went to Chile and climbed some more.

One peak he climbed there was Ojos del Salado. Officially it's 22,800 feet high, but the Chileans say it is taller than Aconcagua. Tejas left an Alaskan flag behind on the summit, something he figured would make a nifty souvenir for the next group of climbers.

In Chile, Tejas had what might have been the biggest scare he had experienced in the whole preceding year. This was a man who had scaled the highest peaks in South America, North America, and Antarctica and soloed all of them without suffering any notable injury. But in Santiago, in a city park, while playing the fiddle, Tejas was attacked by three teenagers seeking money. One carried an iron bar and Tejas lifted his fiddle as a shield and saw it smashed to pieces.

Enraged, Tejas fought back at his attackers. One ran away immediately. Another was knocked to the ground. When people came out of the shadows (he thinks to rescue him), Tejas was on top of the third man, pounding on him.

Once back in Alaska, Tejas was again toasted by fellow climbers.

"Jeez," was the first reaction of Todd Miner, mountaineering instructor at the University of Alaska, Anchorage, who has climbed McKinley. "He's now one of the premier cold-weather climbers in the world."

Harry Johnson, Tejas's employer, said, "It's a neat thing to do in a still relatively unexplored area. We're proud."

And so was Tejas.

"It's a real good feeling that comes to you," he said. "You realize, 'I gave it a good shot and I succeeded and it's mine.' It's the same as if you're a runner: you think, 'Damn, that was a good race.' I did my personal best. But if you put it in the context of the whole universe, it's not that important. It helps me to define myself.

"As far as it being a record for humanity . . . nah. It's sort of like juggling for three days. It probably hasn't been done before, but someone will do it again."

Immediately after Tejas returned to Anchorage, he began planning his next challenge: a climb of 29,028-foot Mount Everest, the world's tallest mountain.

"I'm intimidated," said Tejas. "It's a real big hill."

The biggest hill of all.

Will Tejas solo Everest?

"Are you crazy?" he said.

McKinley, 1989

Mount McKinley was a popular place in winter a year after Tejas's historic climb. Climbers continued to take the dare and assault the continent's tallest and most forbidding peak. McKinley, as one can expect, was not always hospitable.

No one was so daring, or perhaps foolish is the word, as to attempt a winter climb in the middle of winter. No one dares to choose such a dream in December or early January. For one thing, there are only a few hours of daylight, and climbers know if there is a chance for McKinley to be gentle in winter, the chance comes as the season is about to turn to spring on the calendar.

However, in late February, and on into mid-March, McKinley was crowded by winter standards. A team of strong Austrian climbers was working its way up the West Buttress route. Just behind them was a three-member Japanese team. That group included Noboru Yamada, a friend of the deceased Naomi Uemura. Yamada was going for a winter climbing sweep, hoping to become the first person to climb the highest mountain on each of the world's seven continents during the winter.

And on another part of the mountain, Dave Staeheli, a thirty-three-year-old Anchorage mountaineer and professional guide, who is a friend and coworker of Tejas's, was cautiously climbing the West Rib solo. The West Rib is a more technically difficult route than the West Buttress and is not very commonly climbed, even by groups in the summer.

McKinley would have harsh words with each of these climbing parties.

Earlier in the winter, in January, Alaska experienced its coldest temperatures in fifteen years. Even in the Interior, where extreme lows are the norm, daily life came to a standstill. Few could cope with thermometer readings that dipped as low as seventy-five or eighty degrees below zero. Dog mushers training for the Iditarod Trail Sled Dog Race abandoned their homes, moving their dogs by truck to southern parts of the state—where the temperature was only thirty below.

None of these climbers were on the mountain during the cold snap. No one could imagine how cold it must have been on McKinley when the cities were gripped in such an icy hold. Thermometers don't measure temperatures that cold.

These climbers came to the mountain with the hope that the worst of the winter was behind them. And for a time it seemed as if they were right. Then the storms moved in. Just another Mount McKinley temper tantrum, most Alaskans figured when they heard that storms were blasting the mountain. But no winter McKinley storm can be considered routine when men are on the mountain.

The Austrians were the first to emerge. They came off the mountain proud of their success in reaching the summit and with a feeling that they were lucky to survive the brutal weather.

Then word came that Staeheli was all right. He was still on the mountain, still driving for the summit.

But no word from the Japanese. No word from them, and no sign of them, when the skies cleared. If it was clear, there should be movement. The planes went up to look. The bush pilots looked and saw nothing. They looked some more and saw a row of three bright spots contrasting with the snow.

The three bright spots were bodies.

No one knew how the men died. Once again, people could

only guess. This time the speculation centered on not loose crampons but on deadly winds. Park rangers guessed that winds blustering up to 200 miles an hour blew the men off a ridge at Denali Pass at 18,200 feet. Their bodies were found 800 feet below.

McKinley had claimed more victims, more of Japan's finest men. Once more, the Japanese people were anguished. It was not until early April, a few weeks after the climbers had died, that a team of seventeen Japanese climbers carried the bodies of their comrades off the mountain.

Staeheli, a veteran of fifteen previous McKinley climbs (thirteen to the summit), outlasted the mountain's fury. Staeheli knew McKinley well, but he did not know the West Rib at all. He was looking for a new challenge, and this was his first time on the route.

Staeheli sought to make his climb with a minimum of fanfare, but he did discuss it briefly with Tejas. And like Tejas, he was inspired by the attempt Uemura had made five years before.

Since he had climbed McKinley via the West Buttress so frequently, Staeheli said he never considered a solo by that route. He thought for a few years about the West Rib, or even the still-tougher Cassin Ridge, before making his attempt. One reason it took him so long to make the try was his business. The two previous winters, Staeheli was tied up making guided climbs in New Zealand.

"Soloing is extremely rewarding to me," said Staeheli, who has climbed solo on other high Alaska peaks, including Mount Drum and Mount Sanford in the Wrangell–St. Elias Range. "It's one-on-one, just you and the mountain. It requires more concentration, and generally it takes every skill you've got. And if you make the top, it's strictly on your own accomplishments."

The bad weather came early in his climb, but Staeheli said he was never truly pinned down. Each day he advanced some; at least once he actually climbed only for an hour and a half.

"I said, 'Forget this,'" said Staeheli of that day.

Despite the weather and the drama simultaneously going on elsewhere on the mountain, Staeheli did his solo climb in seventeen days. That made him the second man to complete a solo winter climb of Mount McKinley—and live to tell the story of it.

Tejas was thrilled for his friend.

Vern Tejas. **Photo by Lewis Freedman.**

"I'm tickled that Dave did it," he said. "Originally, I had given him a fifty-fifty chance because he chose a very difficult route. I was pretty stoked. He made real progress on the mountain."

Progress. But Tejas knows as well as any other prominent climber that some day, someone traveling alone in winter will take a stab at the Cassin Ridge, the toughest way to the top of them all.

"The door is still open for people to continue," said Tejas.